LSAT®
PrepTest 82
Unlocked

Exclusive Data, Analysis, & Explanations for the
September 2017 LSAT

KAPLAN

PUBLISHING

New York

LSAT® is a registered mark of the Law School Admission Council, Inc.

© 2018 by Kaplan, Inc.

Published by Kaplan Publishing, a division of Kaplan, Inc.
750 Third Avenue
New York, NY 10017

ISBN: 978-1-5062-3907-1
10 9 8 7 6 5 4 3 2 1

Table of Contents

The Inside Story

PrepTest 82 was administered in September 2017. It challenged 27,606 test takers. What made this test so hard? Here's a breakdown of what Kaplan students who were surveyed after taking the official exam considered PrepTest 82's most difficult section.

Hardest PrepTest 82 Section as Reported by Test Takers

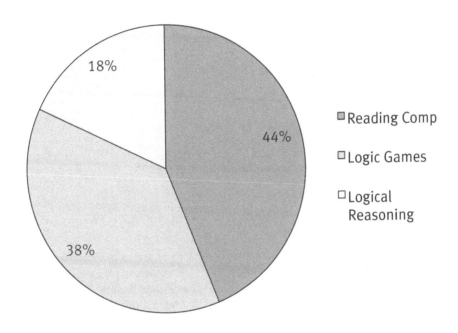

PrepTest 82 is an outlier because a plurality of students considered Reading Comprehension the hardest section on that LSAT. PrepTest 82 is one of only four LSAT administrations since 2010 (and the first since February 2013) where Reading Comprehension was the top vote-getter in the survey. Were you to base you opinion only on these results, you might think that studying Reading Comp is the key to LSAT success. Reading Comp is important, but test takers' perceptions don't tell the whole story: you need to consider students' actual performance. The following chart shows the average number of students to miss each question in each of PrepTest 82's different sections.

Percentage Incorrect by PrepTest 82 Section Type

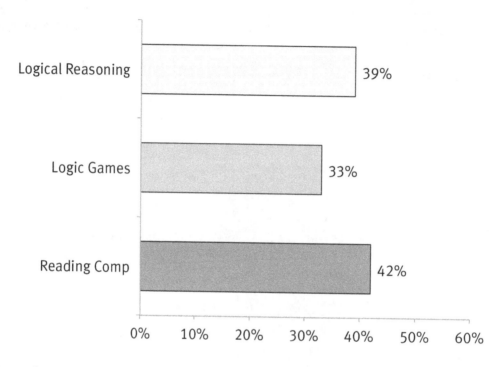

Actual student performance tells quite a different story. On average, Reading Comprehension was indeed the toughest section, but not nearly by the overwhelming margin that "perceived difficulty" suggests—especially in comparison to Logical Reasoning. On most exams, we see a similar disparity between the perceived difficulty of Logic Games and the actual test taker performance in that section. On almost every released LSAT, actual performance results show that the difficulty of sections is relatively equal.

Maybe students overestimate the difficulty of a challenging Logic Games or Reading Comprehension section because a very hard game or passage is so easy to remember after the test. In contrast, it's much harder to remember the hardest Logical Reasoning questions when there are a total of 50 or 51 LR questions on the test. The truth is that the testmaker places hard questions throughout the test, and students striving for a top score want to be prepared for all of them. As tough as the Reading Comprehension section was on PrepTest 82, it contained only four of the exam's ten hardest questions, while six of the ten hardest were in Logical Reasoning. Here were the locations of the 10 hardest (most missed) questions in the exam.

Location of 10 Most Difficult Questions in PrepTest 82

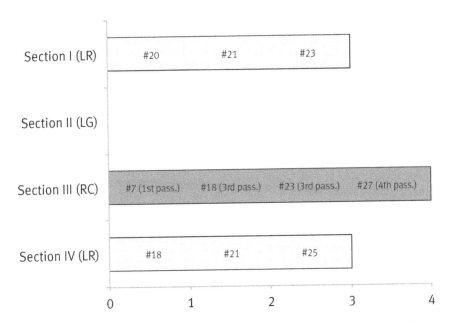

The takeaway from this data is that, to maximize your potential on the LSAT, you need to take a comprehensive approach. Test yourself rigorously, and review your performance on every section of the test. Kaplan's LSAT explanations provide the expertise and insight you need to fully understand your results. The explanations are written and edited by a team of LSAT experts, who have helped thousands of students improve their scores. Kaplan always provides data-driven analysis of the test, ranking the difficulty of every question based on actual student performance. The 10 hardest questions on every test are highlighted with a 4-star difficulty rating, the highest we give. The analysis breaks down the remaining questions into 1-, 2-, and 3-star ratings so that you can compare your performance to thousands of other test takers on all LSAC material.

Don't settle for wondering whether a question was really as hard as it seemed to you. Analyze the test with real data, and learn the secrets and strategies that help top scorers master the LSAT.

7 Can't-Miss Features of PrepTest 82

- Although only five Inference questions in Logical Reasoning is not unheard of, that was just half as many as there were on PT 81.
- As of the release of PT 82, the Logic Games section had only started with a Hybrid game eight times ever, but PT 82 was the first time it had ever happened in back-to-back tests.
- Speaking of that first Hybrid game, it was a Distribution/Sequencing Hybrid. That was the first time those actions have been combined in a Hybrid game since September 2014 (PT 73).
- The Reading Comprehension section nearly always contains a Humanities, Law, Natural Science, and Social Science passage. However, in a rare move, PT 82 omitted a Humanities passage in favor of a second Social Science passage.
- As of its release, PT 82 was only the third LSAT ever—and first since October 2015 (PT 76)—on which a Comparative Reading passage had eight questions.
- If you had to guess on the last question of a section, (E) was your best bet—it was correct three of four times.
- The final logic game involved student presentations on Machiavellianism, jitsuaku, and Shakespeare's villains. Speaking of evil, students may have unwound after the test by watching Pennywise the Dancing Clown in *It*, which was the #1 movie in America the week this test was administered.

PrepTest 82 in Context

As much fun as it is to find out what makes a PrepTest unique or noteworthy, it's even more important to know just how representative it is of other LSAT administrations (and, thus, how likely it is to be representative of the exam you will face on Test Day). The following charts compare the numbers of each kind of question and game on PrepTest 82 to the average numbers seen on all officially released LSATs administered over the past five years (from 2013 through 2017).

Number of LR Questions by Type: PrepTest 82 vs. 2013–2017 Average

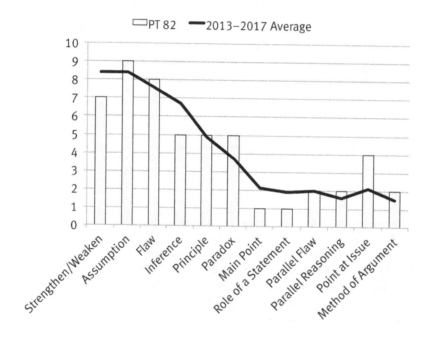

KAPLAN

Number of LG Games by Type: PrepTest 82 vs. 2013–2017 Average

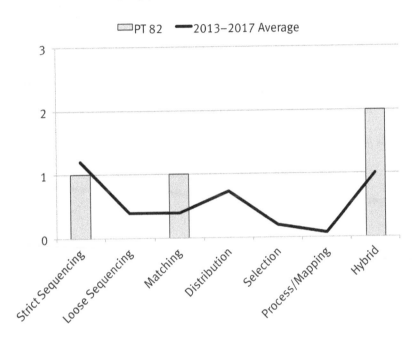

Number of RC Questions by Type: PrepTest 82 vs. 2013–2017 Average

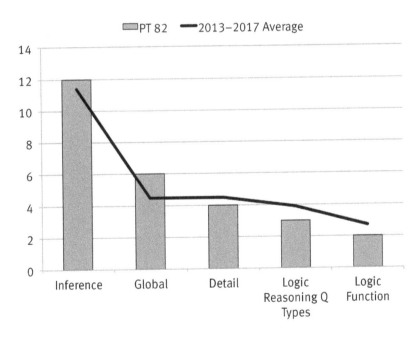

There isn't usually a huge difference in the distribution of questions from LSAT to LSAT, but if this test seems harder (or easier) to you than another you've taken, compare the number of questions of the types on which you, personally, are strongest and weakest. Then, explore within each section to see if your best or worst question types came earlier or later.

Students in Kaplan's comprehensive LSAT courses have access to every released LSAT and to a library of thousands of officially released questions arranged by question, game, and passage type. If you are studying on your own, you have to do a bit more work to identify your strengths and your areas of opportunity. Quantitative analysis (like that in the charts shown here) is an important tool for understanding how the test is constructed, and how you are performing on it.

Section I: Logical Reasoning

Q#	Question Type	Correct	Difficulty
1	Flaw	D	★
2	Point at Issue	A	★
3	Assumption (Sufficient)	C	★
4	Principle (Identify/Strengthen)	E	★
5	Weaken (EXCEPT)	C	★
6	Inference	C	★
7	Assumption (Necessary)	B	★
8	Paradox	B	★
9	Strengthen	C	★★
10	Main Point	E	★★★
11	Flaw	E	★
12	Assumption (Necessary)	B	★★★
13	Paradox	D	★★
14	Principle (Identify/Inference)	D	★★
15	Weaken	A	★★
16	Parallel Flaw	B	★★
17	Paradox	B	★★★
18	Flaw	C	★★
19	Parallel Reasoning	A	★★★
20	Method of Argument	A	★★★★
21	Principle (Apply/Inference)	A	★★★★
22	Flaw	E	★★★★
23	Assumption (Necessary)	A	★★★
24	Inference	C	★★
25	Assumption (Necessary)	E	★★

1. (D) Flaw

Step 1: Identify the Question Type

The correct answer will describe how the argument is "vulnerable to criticism," making this a Flaw question.

Step 2: Untangle the Stimulus

The student concludes ([*t*]*hus*) that newly enacted penalties will be ineffective at reducing on-campus alcohol drinking. The evidence is that previous attempts to reduce such drinking have failed.

Step 3: Make a Prediction

Past experience is not a predictor of future results. As with any prediction, this argument assumes nothing relevant has changed. Perhaps there's something different about the new penalties that will make them more effective. The correct answer will describe this overlooked possibility.

Step 4: Evaluate the Answer Choices

(D) is correct.

(A) is irrelevant. There's no need to describe the specifics of a plan to suggest it won't work.

(B) is irrelevant. Even if many students already don't drink alcohol, that has no bearing on whether the new plan will reduce the number of students who do.

(C) is Out of Scope. Location preference doesn't matter. As long as there's any alcohol drinking on campus, the argument still stands and is flawed for a different reason.

(E) is Out of Scope. Other consequences don't matter. The argument is only about whether the penalties will reduce drinking.

2. (A) Point at Issue

Step 1: Identify the Question Type

There are two speakers and the question asks for something about which they *disagree*, making this a Point at Issue question.

Step 2: Untangle the Stimulus

Anderson argues that we shouldn't worry about violating the rules of grammar because the rules are always changing and evolving. Lipton counters this by drawing an analogy to law enforcement: Laws are always changing, but it's still good to enforce them.

Step 3: Make a Prediction

By claiming that laws should still be enforced, Lipton is implying that we should hold the same standard to grammar: Follow the rules. This is contrary to Anderson's point, so the correct answer will address this issue of whether or not grammar rules should be followed.

Step 4: Evaluate the Answer Choices

(A) is correct. Use the Decision Tree to confirm. Anderson would say no to this: It's okay to violate the rules of grammar.

Lipton would say yes to this: We should resist violating the rules. And most importantly, they do disagree with each other.

(B) is Out of Scope for Lipton. Only Anderson refers to languages evolving into new languages. Lipton only disputes the need to follow the rules, not how drastically languages can evolve.

(C) is Out of Scope. Neither speaker talks about how easy it is for people to adapt to changes.

(D) is Out of Scope. Neither speaker addresses the frequency of grammar violations.

(E) is a 180 at worst. Anderson discusses how languages evolve in this manner. And Lipton's analogy shows how laws can evolve, suggesting agreement (not disagreement) about how language can evolve.

3. (C) Assumption (Sufficient)

Step 1: Identify the Question Type

The author can properly draw the given conclusion *if* the correct answer is *assumed*, making this a Sufficient Assumption question.

Step 2: Untangle the Stimulus

The author begins with the conclusion: Requiring elaborate passwords actually makes it *more* likely that somebody will gain unauthorized access to an account. The evidence is that users often write down complex passwords because they're hard to remember, and entering the wrong password too many times can lock the user out.

Step 3: Make a Prediction

The evidence merely claims that people will tend to write down complex passwords. However, the conclusion makes an unsupported leap to a new concept: an increased likelihood of other people gaining unauthorized access. The author is assuming these concepts are connected—that writing passwords down will somehow lead to an increase in unauthorized access.

Step 4: Evaluate the Answer Choices

(C) is correct. If writing a password down makes unauthorized access more likely, then the author's argument is sound.

(A) is Out of Scope. Even if there are some users who can remember their password in this manner, the argument is based on people who don't do this and often write passwords down.

(B) is irrelevant. It doesn't matter how long it takes locked accounts to become unlocked. This does nothing to confirm the conclusion about increased unauthorized access.

(D) is Out of Scope. How users get back into locked accounts has no bearing on whether unauthorized access will increase or not.

(E) is a 180. If complex passwords are just as easy to guess as simple passwords, then the likelihood of unauthorized access should be equal, not greater. Besides, this makes no connection to the evidence about passwords being written down.

4. (E) Principle (Identify/Strengthen)

Step 1: Identify the Question Type

The correct answer will be a principle, making this an Identify the Principle question. Further, the principle will be used to *justify* the specific argument given, which means this will also work like a Strengthen question.

Step 2: Untangle the Stimulus

The author makes a recommendation: The police chief should be held accountable for corruption in the police department. The reasoning is that the chief has been the department head for a long time. Even a lack of incriminating evidence against the chief is not enough to change the author's mind.

Step 3: Make a Prediction

The author is steadfast in asserting the chief's responsibility. And it's all based on the chief's lengthy tenure. Not even a lack of evidence against the chief changes that. This stubbornness is justified if the author believes that a lengthy tenure in control is enough, by itself, to make one responsible for internal troubles.

Step 4: Evaluate the Answer Choices

(E) is correct. The chief has been the head for a long time, and this principle justifies the recommendation of holding the chief responsible.

(A) is Out of Scope. There is no indication that the chief "knowingly tolerates" the corruption, so it's impossible to know if this principle would apply.

(B) is Extreme. The corruption is said to be widespread, but there's no evidence that *all* of the chief's subordinates are corrupt. And even if they were, this only suggests the chief *knew* about the corruption. There's nothing here about being held responsible.

(C) is Out of Scope. There's no indication whether or not the chief "could reasonably be expected" to have known about the corruption. Without that information, there's no way to know if this principle would apply.

(D) is Out of Scope. The argument is not about whether one should take corrective action or not. And this principle only applies if the person in charge is *not* in charge for long, unlike the chief.

5. (C) Weaken (EXCEPT)

Step 1: Identify the Question Type

The question asks for information that would "call into question" a given argument. That makes this a Weaken

question. However, the word EXCEPT indicates that four choices will weaken the argument. The correct answer will be the one that does *not*—it will either strengthen the argument or have no effect.

Step 2: Untangle the Stimulus

A store was being vandalized, so the owner told a friend about a plan to install bright lighting around the store's perimeter. Three months later, the vandalism had stopped. The friend concluded that the owner installed the lighting.

Step 3: Make a Prediction

Perimeter lighting might have been good enough to reduce the vandalism. However, reduced vandalism does not necessarily indicate perimeter lighting was installed. Other actions could have produced the same result. Because the friend insists there was perimeter lighting, any choices that indicate or suggest an alternative explanation would weaken the argument.

Step 4: Evaluate the Answer Choices

(C) is correct, as it could possibly strengthen the friend's argument. This claims that vandalism went down only in the area near the store's perimeter and not elsewhere. That suggests something changed in that area, perhaps the installation of bright lighting.

(A) raises an alternate possibility (more police), and thus weakens the likelihood of perimeter lighting being the cause.

(B) weakens the argument by suggesting the owner didn't have time to install bright lighting. The conversation was only three months ago, so there is more likely to be another explanation for the drop in vandalism.

(D) weakens the argument. If the owner couldn't afford bright lighting, then there is likely to be another explanation for the drop in vandalism.

(E) raises an alternate possibility (a watchdog), and thus weakens the likelihood that perimeter lighting was the cause.

6. (C) Inference

Step 1: Identify the Question Type

The correct answer will be "supported by" the information provided, making this an Inference question.

Step 2: Untangle the Stimulus

The author presents some research results. When competing, athletes who play for the love of the game have sharper vision than those whose primary goal is winning. This is because sharper vision requires concentration that is more prevalent in people focused on the activity itself.

Step 3: Make a Prediction

The Keyword *because* indicates a cause-and-effect relationship. Here, a greater focus on the activity itself is said to produce the concentration needed for sharp vision, and that causes people who play for the love of the game to have sharper vision. The implication is that people who play for the love of the game are more focused on the activity itself than people who play primarily to win.

Step 4: Evaluate the Answer Choices
(C) is directly supported.

(A) is a Distortion. Athletes who play mainly for the love of the game are distinguished from those whose *main* goal is winning. That doesn't mean those who play for the love of the game don't want to win. It's just not their *main* goal.

(B) is a Distortion. The statements discuss conditions necessary for *acute* vision, not *adequate* vision.

(D) is an Extreme Distortion. Some athletes may be focused on the activity itself, but that's not to say it's *impossible* for other athletes to have divided attention.

(E) is Extreme and Out of Scope. Focused attention provides concentration that is *necessary*, but that doesn't mean it *will* lead to better results. Besides, the author never claims that those with "acute vision" will necessarily "perform better."

7. (B) Assumption (Necessary)

Step 1: Identify the Question Type
The question asks for something the given argument "requires assuming," making this a Necessary Assumption question.

Step 2: Untangle the Stimulus
The economist concludes ([*s*]*o*) that ChesChem will move manufacturing to Tilsen if natural gas prices in Chester go up. The evidence is that natural gas currently costs twice as much in Chester as it does in Tilsen, and ChesChem will move manufacturing to Tilsen if the cost in Chester is more than twice as much.

Step 3: Make a Prediction
As the economist suggests, an increase in gas prices in Chester would make it more than double the price in Tilsen, which would logically prompt the move to Tilsen . . . unless the price of gas also goes up in Tilsen. If the price in Tilsen goes up, then the price could go up in Chester without exceeding the "twice as much" condition. Then, the company wouldn't necessarily move. So, the economist must assume that the price of gas in Tilsen won't go up, guaranteeing a move if Chester prices rise.

Step 4: Evaluate the Answer Choices
(B) is correct. Using the Denial Test, if the price of gas in Tilsen *does* increase, then higher prices in Chester wouldn't necessarily bring about the condition for moving, and the economist's conclusion is no longer valid. So, the economist must assume that won't happen.

(A) is an Irrelevant Comparison. The argument depends solely on the price of natural gas, not the cost of any other expense.

(C) is Out of Scope. The argument is only about staying in Chester or moving to Tilsen. Profits are not a factor here.

(D) is Extreme. Lower costs need not be the *only* benefit of moving to Tilsen. Even if there were *other* benefits, the argument would be unaffected.

(E) is a Distortion. The conclusion is that *if* costs increased, ChesChem would move. That means increased costs are sufficient—they would guarantee the move. However, that's not to say the price *must* increase (i.e., it's necessary). It's possible ChesChem could move for other reasons, even if gas costs don't increase.

8. (B) Paradox

Step 1: Identify the Question Type
The correct answer will *explain* a behavior. If it has to be explained, it will probably seem unusual, making this a Paradox question.

Step 2: Untangle the Stimulus
Cuttlefish have a behavior called a "startle display," which involves making themselves look larger. The assumption was that this was used to scare off predators. However, a study showed cuttlefish only used it to scare off smaller fish, not predators.

Step 3: Make a Prediction
If the smaller fish don't prey on the cuttlefish, why scare them off? Don't bother trying to predict a specific explanation. Just anticipate that the correct answer will describe a benefit to scaring off the smaller fish.

Step 4: Evaluate the Answer Choices
(B) is correct. This suggests that cuttlefish are scaring off the small fish so that they don't attract larger predators that would pose a threat to the cuttlefish.

(A) is a 180. If cuttlefish eat small fish, it makes even less sense that they would scare such fish away.

(C) is an Irrelevant Comparison. Even if it's easier to scare the small fish, there's still no benefit to doing so, and there's no explanation why they wouldn't at least try scaring away predators when the alternative is to be eaten.

(D) is irrelevant. Acute senses and color-changing have nothing to do with why cuttlefish scare away small fish.

(E) addresses the wrong question. If cuttlefish are faster than their predators, that might explain why they *don't* need to use the startle display on predators. However, the question is why they *do* use the startle display on small fish, and this offers no explanation for that.

9. (C) Strengthen

Step 1: Identify the Question Type
The question directly asks for something that "strengthens the argument," making this a Strengthen question.

Step 2: Untangle the Stimulus
The author is arguing that the lottery in question did not meet the fairness requirement, which is that all entrants have an equal chance of winning. The evidence is that people had 30 days to enter, but 90% of the winners were people who entered during just the first two days.

Step 3: Make a Prediction
The author is implying that not everyone had an equal chance of winning. And the statistics certainly suggest that people who entered within the first two days had a *much* better chance. However, why did so many people from that group win? Was there really some unfair advantage? Or is it possible that most people entered during the first two days, and there just weren't a lot of entrants after that? The author assumes some sort of unfair advantage, and the correct answer will validate that enough people entered on days 3–30 to suggest the results were improperly skewed.

Step 4: Evaluate the Answer Choices
(C) is correct. If entry forms were submitted consistently, then the winning entries should have been a little more evenly distributed over the 30-day period, not weighted 9 to 1 in favor of early entrants. That makes the author's accusation seem more justified.

(A) is Out of Scope. The argument is about the lopsided results for people who *did* enter. It doesn't matter who could and who couldn't participate.

(B) is irrelevant. Publicizing the selection process ahead of time makes it no more or less likely that it was a fair process. If anything, it contradicts the author. If it was publicized beforehand, then everyone would have had access to that knowledge, giving everyone an equal opportunity to know the best way of winning.

(D) is a 180 at worst. This states the rules were made clear, suggesting that details weren't hidden from people such that it would affect their chances of winning.

(E) is irrelevant. It doesn't matter how many people entered in total. What matters is *when* they entered. If almost all of these people (say, 90% of them) entered in the first two days, then the author's argument is invalid.

10. (E) Main Point

Step 1: Identify the Question Type
The question asks for the "main conclusion drawn," making this a Main Point question.

Step 2: Untangle the Stimulus
Godinez is arguing about how land is measured. In the past, land was measured by how long it took to plow. However, that doesn't help when the land is used for other reasons such as housing apartment complexes. *Therefore*, Godinez concludes that as people developed more uses for land, they needed to develop new ways to measure it.

Step 3: Make a Prediction
While there are two conclusion keywords here ([*t*]*hus* and [*t*]*herefore*), the first one is just used to clarify how plowing time was used to measure land in the past. After [*h*]*owever*, Godinez shifts the scope and moves on to the bigger point: Things have changed. And with new uses for land, people needed new ways to measure it. That's the conclusion at the end, and it's the main point supported by the details before it.

Step 4: Evaluate the Answer Choices
(E) expresses Godinez's main point.

(A) is a Distortion. Godinez argues we needed to switch to a new measure such as acreage, but never suggests that it's *easier*.

(B) is a Distortion. Godinez never makes any claim about accuracy. It's just that newer measures are more relevant. And even accepting that, a claim of greater accuracy and/or greater relevance would merely be evidence for the point that a change was needed, not the main point itself.

(C) is the wrong point. This might sway readers who stopped after finding the Keyword [*t*]*hus*. However, when Godinez uses the Keyword [*h*]*owever*, that changes the focus of the argument to how things have changed. The measurement tactic described in this statement is no longer appropriate.

(D) is a Distortion. In the conclusion, Godinez merely says it became necessary to adopt new measures. Godinez never actually says *when* those new measures were actually adopted. And the need for new measures arose from diversification of land use, not people's realization of the inadequacy of using plowing time.

11. (E) Flaw

Step 1: Identify the Question Type
The correct answer will describe why "the argument is flawed," making this a Flaw question.

Step 2: Untangle the Stimulus
The author argues that measures to clean up the Lalolah River must be working. The evidence is that, of a group of 15 rivers, the Lalolah River was ranked the most polluted last year but only third most polluted this year.

Step 3: Make a Prediction
Unfortunately, there are two ways to move down the list. One is what the author suggests: The Lalolah River is cleaner and

now less polluted than two other rivers. However, there is an Overlooked Possibility: The Lalolah River might be just as polluted, but two other rivers got *worse* and are now ranked higher. Ranking is relative, and the correct answer will point out the author's failure to consider that.

Step 4: Evaluate the Answer Choices

(E) is correct. The author suggests that a "decrease relative to the other ranked rivers" (Lalolah went from most polluted to third most) is the same as "an absolute decrease" (it became less polluted), and that's not necessarily true. Other rivers could just have become more polluted.

(A) is not accurate. This suggests the author claimed "the plan is working because there's no evidence it's *not* working." However, the author does have evidence but interprets it incorrectly.

(B) suggests equivocation, but the phrase "most polluted" is not ambiguous here. It means "more polluted than any of the other rivers," and there's no confusion about that.

(C) is irrelevant. The specific basis doesn't matter. If it's cleaner, it's cleaner, regardless of the particular method used for measuring that.

(D) is Out of Scope. The argument is only about individual river pollution levels. The state of the district as a whole has no bearing on this argument.

12. (B) Assumption (Necessary)

Step 1: Identify the Question Type

The question asks for an "assumption required by the argument," making this a Necessary Assumption question.

Step 2: Untangle the Stimulus

The author concludes ([*thus*]) that doctors should be prepared to discuss yoga with patients experiencing chronic lower back pain. The evidence is that doctors should be prepared to discuss an activity if it significantly reduces chronic lower back pain, and studies show that yoga reduces such pain as much as a stretching class with a physical therapist does.

Step 3: Make a Prediction

By the first sentence, to conclude that doctors should prepare to discuss yoga, the author must assume that yoga can significantly reduce chronic lower back pain. However, it's only said that yoga reduces such pain "as much as training classes do." So, the author must assume that training classes reduce a significant amount of pain; otherwise, the argument doesn't work.

Step 4: Evaluate the Answer Choices

(B) must be assumed. Using the Denial Test, if stretching classes did *not* significantly reduce chronic lower back pain and yoga was the same, then there's no significant reduction and no need to discuss it. That would destroy the argument,

so the author must assume these activities *do* significantly reduce such pain.

(A) is an Irrelevant Comparison. The argument is that doctors should be prepared to discuss *any* activity if it's significantly effective. The availability of other, more effective options is irrelevant.

(C) is not necessary. It doesn't matter how many options are available. All that matters is whether or not yoga can significantly reduce chronic lower back pain.

(D) is not necessary. It doesn't matter if the study cited is the first or the millionth of its kind. All that matters are the results.

(E) is a Distortion. It doesn't matter if doctors actually discuss stretching classes or not. As long as such classes significantly reduce chronic lower back pain and doctors are *prepared* to discuss those classes, the argument still stands.

13. (D) Paradox

Step 1: Identify the Question Type

Although there are two speakers, the question asks for something that will "resolve the apparent conflict" between their claims. That makes this a Paradox question, unlike Point at Issue questions that would ask about a point of disagreement between them.

Step 2: Untangle the Stimulus

Shelton describes a region in which the moose population decreased as the white-tailed deer population increased. The decline in moose is caused by a parasite that the deer carry and pass along to moose. Russo, however, described another region in which the white-tailed deer population increased, but the moose population remained constant.

Step 3: Make a Prediction

The mystery is this: If both regions saw an increase in parasite-carrying deer, why did only one region experience a decline in moose? It's not worth predicting a specific solution. Instead, expect that the answer will provide a reason why the one group of moose was more susceptible to the parasite.

Step 4: Evaluate the Answer Choices

(D) is correct. Where the moose population dropped, they roamed the same area as the deer and were more likely to be exposed to the parasite. Where the moose population didn't change, they didn't cross paths with the deer and were thus spared exposure to the parasite.

(A) is irrelevant. Even if the second region was smaller and had fewer moose, the parasite still should have affected what moose were there.

(B) is a 180. This suggests that the moose in the first territory had better living conditions, yet they *still* had a worse fate than the other moose. The mystery is unsolved.

(C) may offer a reason why moose are even more in peril in the first region. However, it still doesn't explain why moose in the second region didn't decline at all despite the increase in parasite-carrying deer.

(E) is Out of Scope. Neither speaker mentions the level of human settlement in either region, so this offers no explanation for the different moose statistics.

14. (D) Principle (Identify/Inference)

Step 1: Identify the Question Type
The question asks for a *proposition*, which indicates a Principle question. And that principle will be "illustrated by the statements" provided, which means it will be directly supported by what's given, making this akin to an Inference question.

Step 2: Untangle the Stimulus
The author notes how computers are no longer just a luxury in schools and can be used to provide students with skills they'll need to be competitive. However, the author also notes that an emphasis on teaching computer skills has led to a decrease in teaching basic skills such as reading and math.

Step 3: Make a Prediction
A principle will apply the same logic to a broader context. So, it's not just about computer skills. As schools start to shift their focus to teaching new skills, they wind up cutting back on other skills. The correct answer will fit this pattern of increasing one thing at the expense of others.

Step 4: Evaluate the Answer Choices
(D) is a match. Schools are shifting focus to keep pace with current trends and are neglecting some skills (math and reading) in favor or others (computer skills).

(A) is an Irrelevant Comparison. The author only says that one skill is starting to replace the other. The author never argues whether either set of skills is "more valuable."

(B) is Extreme. It just so happens that schools are starting to neglect basic skills, but that doesn't mean schools *cannot* avoid that problem. Perhaps they just haven't figured out how to do it yet.

(C) is Extreme. The author never suggests anything about performing a "complete rethinking" of any subjects.

(E) is Extreme and a Distortion. Technology is important, but it's never said it should be the *primary* goal of education. Besides, the author never makes any recommendation of what *should* be the case. The author only describes the current situation.

15. (A) Weaken

Step 1: Identify the Question Type
The question directly asks for something that would weaken the argument.

Step 2: Untangle the Stimulus
The author concludes ([A]*herefore*) that the gold in certain artifacts was dug from a particular mine in Asia. The evidence is that gold samples from both the artifacts and the mine have very similar trace-element ratios, and those ratios are unlike the ones found in any other known mine.

Step 3: Make a Prediction
Because of the trace-element data, the author makes a good case that the gold couldn't come from another mine. However, that still doesn't mean the gold had to be dug directly from the Asian mine. Perhaps the gold did originate in the mine, but was transported elsewhere before people found it. In short, the correct answer will show how the gold in question did not necessarily have to be dug directly from the Asian mine.

Step 4: Evaluate the Answer Choices
(A) weakens the argument by offering an alternative source for the gold: nearby rivers. So, even though the gold did come from the mine in question, it's possible the gold was gathered by panning the rivers and not from digging in the mine.

(B) is a 180. This suggests the people who created the artifacts also operated the mine in question, which makes it highly likely the author is correct: The gold *was* dug from that mine.

(C) is irrelevant. It doesn't matter when people *started* digging in that mine. If there was still gold to be found centuries later, that gold could have been dug up to create the artifacts.

(D) is irrelevant. The author is not saying the gold was dug *directly* for the more recent artifacts. Even if it was first used in earlier artifacts, the gold could still be originally dug from the mine in question.

(E) is irrelevant. The author is not arguing that gold from the mine was used exclusively for the artifacts. Even if a lot of that dug-up gold was exported, some of it still could have been used to make the artifacts.

16. (B) Parallel Flaw

Step 1: Identify the Question Type
The correct answer will be an argument with reasoning "most similar to that" in the given argument. Further, that reasoning is said to be *flawed*, making this a Parallel Flaw question.

Step 2: Untangle the Stimulus
Most pet owners taking allergy medication are allergic to pets. The author concludes ([A]*herefore*) that pet owner Chuck will likely take allergy medication if he becomes allergic to pets.

Step 3: Make a Prediction

The author illicitly reverses a *most* statement. When it's said that "Most X who have characteristic Y are Z," that doesn't mean "Most X, if they have Z are Y" or "X with Z are likely to be Y." That shifts the makeup of the group. Consider this: The argument says that most pet owners (X) taking allergy medication (Y) are allergic to pets (Z). So, if 1,000 pet owners take allergy medication, then over 500 of those people are allergic to pets. However, there could be thousands upon thousands (even millions) of people allergic to pets (Z) who *don't* take allergy medication (~Y). So, even if Chuck is a pet owner who does become allergic (an X with Z), there's no way to know if he'll take medication or not (Y or ~Y). The correct answer will commit the same error: Present "most X, with characteristic Y are Z," and then change the group to suggest that "if something is X with Z, then it is likely to be Y."

Note: Rather than dealing with this question algebraically, it's also possible to use another structural component to eliminate answers. The conclusion is a positive conditional prediction. If something happens, then another event is likely to happen. The conclusion of **(A)** is a current assertion, not a prediction. The conclusion of **(C)** is about what likely *won't* happen. And the conclusion of **(D)** is about what is *unlikely* to happen. At worst, you'd have to guess between **(B)** and **(E)**.

Step 4: Evaluate the Answer Choices

(B) is a match. A "most X, who have characteristic Y are Z" claim is presented: Most cars (X) taken to Acme (Y) have electrical problems (Z). The author then illicitly suggests that if an X who has Z (if Anastasia's car has electrical problems), it's likely to be Y (taken to Acme). There could be thousands (or even millions) of cars with electrical problems that are *not* taken to Acme.

(A) is not flawed and thus does not match. If "most X who have Y are Z," then something that is X that has Y *is* likely to be Z. So, if most cars taken to Acme have electrical problems, then it *is* logical to assume that Anastasia's car (which was taken to Acme) has electrical problems.

(C) does not match the evidence. This claims that "most X with characteristic Y are *not* Z": Most cars (X) at Acme (Y) do *not* have electrical problems (~Z). However, Anastasia's car *does* have that problem (Z). That's a different argument altogether.

(D) does not match either. This does have similar evidence because it claims that "most X with characteristic Y are Z": Most cars (X) at Acme (Y) have electrical problems (Z). However, its conclusion indicates that Anastasia's car is *not* Z (it does *not* have electrical problems). That's a different argument.

(E) makes a subtle scope shift that makes it incorrect. Its first sentence is identical to that of correct answer **(B)**. So, it

appropriately indicates "most X with characteristic Y are Z." The conclusion is also structured identically to **(B)**—*except* its conditional is *not* that Anastasia's car *has* electrical problems, but rather that Anastasia *thinks* it has electrical problems. That's enough to upend the logic from being parallel to the stimulus. It's not that Chuck *thinks* he has a pet allergy, he actually does develop one.

17. (B) Paradox

Step 1: Identify the Question Type

The correct answer will *explain* what happens in the stimulus, making this a Paradox question.

Step 2: Untangle the Stimulus

According to the scientist, researchers often examine data to look for errors, and then they fix those errors. *However*, the scientist has noticed that most corrections in her field happen to make the data conform closer to one theory in particular (Jones's).

Step 3: Make a Prediction

The mystery here is, why are these corrections all favoring one particular theory? The likelihood is that there's some bias toward Jones's theory, be it intentional or unintentional. It's not worth predicting exactly what's going on, but expect the correct answer to describe how the researchers' examinations could be biased toward Jones's theory.

Step 4: Evaluate the Answer Choices

(B) is correct. If researchers pay more attention to data that conflicts with Jones's theory, then that's where more corrections will be made—correcting data to better conform with Jones's theory. And when the data is already consistent with Jones's theory, the researchers pay less attention and thus likely make fewer corrections.

(A) is a 180, at worst. If all data is given equal weight, then it's harder to understand why they would make more corrections in favor of the theory than against it.

(C) is Out of Scope. There's no discussion here of which lines of research any researchers want to pursue, and it's unclear whether Jones's theory is one they accept.

(D) is irrelevant. This merely suggests that researchers may occasionally miss some errors. But that still doesn't explain why most of the errors they *do* fix tend to favor one theory over others.

(E) is a 180, at worst. If researchers have their own theories, then it's more of a mystery why they mostly correct data to fit Jones's theory and not their own.

18. (C) Flaw

Step 1: Identify the Question Type
The correct answer will describe why the argument is "vulnerable to criticism," common language that indicates a Flaw question.

Step 2: Untangle the Stimulus
The doctor concludes ([*therefore*) that disease X causes high blood pressure. The evidence is that disease X causes increased angiotensinogen levels, and people with higher angiotensinogen levels tend to have higher blood pressure.

Step 3: Make a Prediction
This is a prime example of one of the most commonly tested flaws: correlation versus causation. Disease X causes angiotensinogen levels to rise, but are increased angiotensinogen levels the cause of higher blood pressure? Maybe. However, it's just said that angiotensinogen levels and blood pressure levels coincide. There are three potential flaws: 1) There could be a third factor that causes high blood pressure or perhaps causes both higher angiotensinogen levels and high blood pressure. 2) The doctor could have the logic backward. Perhaps having high blood pressure causes increased angiotensinogen levels (or causes disease X, which in turn causes increased angiotensinogen levels). 3) It could just be a coincidence, and no one thing causes the other. The correct answer will describe one of these three flaws.

Step 4: Evaluate the Answer Choices
(C) describes this classic flaw. It could be all a coincidence. The angiotensinogen levels and blood pressure levels are just correlated; there's no one thing causing the other.

(A) mentions the commonly tested flaw of necessity versus sufficiency. However, that only occurs when there's Formal Logic, and there are no necessary conditions presented.

(B) is irrelevant. If the doctor is right and disease X *does* cause high blood pressure, it wouldn't matter if another factor existed that could neutralize the high blood pressure. The disease would still be a cause of high blood pressure in the first place.

(D) tries to suggest the doctor reversed the logic. However, there's no evidence that disease X definitely causes high blood pressure or that high blood pressure definitely causes disease X. If neither of those claims is given, then the doctor can't confuse one for the other.

(E) is a Distortion and practically a 180. It is given that one phenomenon (disease X) causes a second (higher angiotensinogen levels), but it's never actually given that the second causes a third (high blood pressure). Only a correlation is given. Besides, even if one *does* assume a causal relationship, this claims that the doctor assumes the first phenomenon (disease X) *cannot* cause the third (high

blood pressure), which is the complete opposite of the doctor's conclusion.

19. (A) Parallel Reasoning

Step 1: Identify the Question Type
The correct answer will be an argument that is "most similar in its pattern of reasoning" to the argument given, making this a Parallel Reasoning question.

Step 2: Untangle the Stimulus
The author concludes ([*therefore*) that not all tarantulas have poison fangs. The evidence is that no animal with poison fangs is a good pet, but some tarantulas *are* good pets.

Step 3: Make a Prediction
The logic here is solid, but could use some translation. Start with the one absolute piece of Formal Logic: No creature with poison fangs makes a good pet. This can be translated as:

$$\textbf{If} \quad \textbf{\textit{good pet}} \quad \rightarrow \quad \textbf{\textit{\~{} poison fangs}}$$

This could also be translated as "if it has poison fangs, it's not a good pet," but that's not as helpful here. That's because it's given that some tarantulas *are* good pets, which would thus logically imply that they don't have poison fangs. And that's the conclusion. If not all tarantulas have poison fangs, then *some* of them must *not* have poison fangs.

The correct answer will follow this same format. There will be one piece of absolute Formal Logic (if X, then not Y). It will be given that some Z are X, and the author will conclude that some Z are not Y (i.e., not all Z are Y).

Step 4: Evaluate the Answer Choices
(A) is a match. One piece of absolute Formal Logic is given: If it's written in a regular meter (X), then it cannot be Strawn's (not Y).

$$\textbf{If} \quad \begin{array}{c}\textbf{\textit{regular meter}} \\ \textbf{\textit{(X)}}\end{array} \quad \rightarrow \quad \begin{array}{c}\textbf{\textit{\~{} Strawn's}} \\ \textbf{\textit{(\~{}Y)}}\end{array}$$

Then another piece of evidence: Some poems in the collection (Z) are written in a regular meter (X). And finally a parallel conclusion: Some of those poems (Z) are not written by Strawn (not Y).

(B) does not match. Each statement is about *some* items, and there's no absolute Formal Logic claim.

(C) has parallel evidence, but not a parallel conclusion. The evidence contains one statement of absolute Formal Logic: If Strawn wrote it (X), then it's not in the collection (not Y), and it's given that some poems with regular meter (Z) are written by Strawn (X). So far, so good. However, the conclusion is about poems that *are* in the collection (Y) and how some of them do *not* have regular meter (*not* Z), i.e., some Y are not Z.

That's not the same conclusion structure as the stimulus. In order to be parallel, **(C)** needed to conclude that *some* poems with regular meter (Z) are *not* in the collection (not Y), i.e., some Z are not Y.

(D) is Extreme. The conclusion is pure logic (*only*), and not just about some items.

(E) does not match. The evidence is two pieces of Formal Logic, with no *some* statement.

20. (A) Method of Argument

Step 1: Identify the Question Type

The word *by* indicates the question is asking *how* Varela responds (i.e., by what method), making this a Method of Argument question.

Step 2: Untangle the Stimulus

Pulford argues that if scientists want to study human remains of historical figures for health purposes, they need to consider whether that research is motivated by science or by mere curiosity. Pulford believes only science-based motives are acceptable. Varela points out something Pulford ignores: Legitimate science often comes from curiosity-based research.

Step 3: Make a Prediction

Pulford wants to separate science-based research and curiosity-based research, and Varela points out that science and curiosity are not as separate as Pulford believes. The correct answer will describe Varela's method of pointing out what Pulford overlooks.

Step 4: Evaluate the Answer Choices

(A) is correct. Pulford believes that science-based research and curiosity-based research are distinct, and Varela points out that such a distinction is untenable (i.e., not justified).

(B) is a Distortion. Pulford's principle is that private investigations should only be done for science-based reasons. Varela does not dispute that. Instead, she points out that curiosity-based research could result in science-based research and that curiosity-based research need not violate Pulford's principle.

(C) is Out of Scope. Varela argues with generalizations of her own. No specific counterexamples are provided.

(D) is a 180. It's Pulford that treats two views as separate and Varela who tries to argue they can be seen as one.

(E) is a Distortion. There's nothing inconsistent with Pulford's claims. Pulford just tries to keep two things separate that need not be separated, according to Varela.

21. (A) Principle (Apply/Inference)

Step 1: Identify the Question Type

The question requires taking "principles cited" in the stimulus and using them to "justify the reasoning" in the correct answer. So, this is an Apply the Principle question, and the correct answer will be justified or supported by what's given, making this work like an Inference question.

Step 2: Untangle the Stimulus

The stimulus consists of two principles, both of which use Formal Logic. In the first, the phrase "only if" indicates a necessary condition for revealing a secret: If it's morally right, then the person revealing the secret must be legally obligated *and* cannot be harmed by the reveal. In the second, the word *if* appears twice, indicating a dual sufficient condition: If one promises to keep the secret *and* revealing the secret can harm others, then revealing is morally wrong.

Step 3: Make a Prediction

It helps to put both statements into symbolic form, along with the contrapositives. For the first:

If	**morally right to reveal**	→	**legal obligation AND ~ harm self**
If	**~ legal obligation OR harm self**	→	**~ morally right to reveal**

For the second:

If	**promise to keep AND can hurt others**	→	**morally wrong to reveal**
If	**~ morally wrong to reveal**	→	**~ promise to keep OR will ~ hurt others**

The correct answer must follow the Formal Logic properly, without illicitly reversing or negating the logic.

Step 4: Evaluate the Answer Choices

(A) is correct. The ultimate point is that Kathryn was not legally obligated to reveal the secret. And, by the first principle, one must be legally obligated for it to be morally right. Since Kathryn wasn't obligated, it wasn't morally right.

(B) is a 180. By the first principle, there must be a legal obligation. The attorney here was not legally obligated, so it was not morally right.

(C) is not supported. There's no information about legal obligation or harm to Judy herself, so the first principle doesn't apply. As for the sufficient part of the second principle, it's possible Judy's action may have hurt her father ("sometimes . . . inhibits recovery"). However, that doesn't rise to the level of "*likely* to result in any harm to others." Further, Judy didn't promise to keep the secret, so the first part of the second principle's sufficient term was not triggered either; thus, the second principle doesn't apply. Hence, there is no information that would validate a finding that Judy's action was morally wrong.

(D) is a 180. To be morally right, Phil would have to be legally obligated (which he was) *and* he couldn't harm himself. However, it's stated that he *did* put himself in danger, so that contradicts the principle.

(E) is Out of Scope. The principles are based on judging people who *do* reveal secrets. The journalist did *not* reveal secrets, so neither of the principles applies.

22. (E) Flaw

Step 1: Identify the Question Type
The correct answer will be the one that "describes a flaw" in the argument, making this a Flaw question.

Step 2: Untangle the Stimulus
The author starts with the conclusion: The first economies were based on bartering, and money came later. The evidence for this (indicated by the phrase "[t]his can be inferred from") is that there have been occasions when certain societies stopped using money and reverted back to their original barter system until money became available again.

Step 3: Make a Prediction
So, the evidence involves societies that ran out of money. They moved to a barter system, which makes sense when there's no money. However, the author claims these societies reverted back to their *original* barter system. That assumes societies started with bartering in the first place . . . which is the conclusion. In other words, in order to conclude that bartering came first, the author has to assume that bartering came first. This is what is known as circular reasoning, and the correct answer will describe this flaw.

Step 4: Evaluate the Answer Choices
(E) is correct. The conclusion that bartering came first relies on the premise that cashless societies reverted to their original barter system . . . which assumes that bartering came first.

(A) is Out of Scope. The conclusion makes no claim of causality, and there is nothing described as *necessary* in the evidence.

(B) is a 180. There is no claim that contradicts another claim. Everything is consistent, as long as the author's assumption is correct.

(C) is Out of Scope. There is no recommendation of what should be done.

(D) is a Distortion. The author does claim that one thing (barter system) occurred before another (currency system). However, the conclusion is not that one system *caused* the other to come about.

23. (A) Assumption (Necessary)

Step 1: Identify the Question Type
The question directly asks for an assumption on which the argument *depends*, making this a Necessary Assumption question.

Step 2: Untangle the Stimulus
The author mentions a study that supposedly provides evidence for the conclusion that crows can recognize threatening people and pass that information to other crows. In the study, researchers wore rubber caveman masks, trapped a bunch of crows, then released them. Years later, people went to the same area, wearing the same masks, and were attacked by crows.

Step 3: Make a Prediction
First, take a moment to stop laughing at how ridiculous this whole situation is . . . Better? Good. Let's proceed. The fact that crows started attacking the masked people is surely a sign of recognition. ("Hey! I've seen that caveman mask before. You're not going to trap us this time!") However, the conclusion is that the crows recognize the threat *and pass that information to other crows*. If the masked people were only attacked by the same crows that were previously trapped, that part of the conclusion doesn't work. The only way this argument works is if some of those crows were different and had been warned by the others. That's the assumption.

Step 4: Evaluate the Answer Choices
(A) is correct. If the attacking birds were all trapped before, then there's no evidence that the crows pass the information along. The author must assume that some of the attacking birds were *not* originally trapped.

(B) is Extreme. The crows don't *always* have to respond the same way. They could respond by staring menacingly or sneaking up behind people and dropping worms in their hair, and the argument wouldn't change.

(C) is Out of Scope. Other bird species are not relevant to the argument, so this behavior need not have any effect on them.

(D) is a 180. This suggests that dive-bombing and shrieking are normal behaviors for crows that see caveman masks. It has nothing to do with them recognizing their captors.

(E) is Half-Right/Half-Wrong, and thus all wrong. Being able to distinguish masked versus non-masked people is helpful, as it would support the idea of recognition. However, there's still no support that crows can pass along the information. Further, there's no need to assume that crows can't distinguish individual faces.

24. (C) Inference

Step 1: Identify the Question Type

The correct answer will be based directly on the statements provided, making this an Inference question. However, while most Inference questions ask for what's supported or true, the correct answer here "must be false," which means the four incorrect choices will all be possible, if not definitely true.

Step 2: Untangle the Stimulus

The first two claims are very noncommittal. When a legislative body gets a bill, most representatives are *usually* ready to vote on it. And if a bill is unlikely to get majority approval, a successful compromise can *usually* be made. However, the last claim is absolute: If a bill is important to a large group of representatives, successful compromise is impossible.

Step 3: Make a Prediction

Because the first two claims describe what's *usually* true, they allow for exceptional cases, which makes it unlikely they'll prove any statement absolutely false. However, the last statement is pure Formal Logic. If a large bloc finds a bill really important, then successful compromise is impossible. A false statement would likely describe such a bill and suggest that successful compromise *is* possible. Even without predicting that, remember that four answers all *could* be true, even if they're not guaranteed. If there's any chance at all that the statement is true, eliminate that choice.

Step 4: Evaluate the Answer Choices

(C) is correct. This mentions bills concerning issues important to large blocs of representatives. By the last claim in the stimulus, successful compromise on such bills is impossible, completely contradictory to the claim here.

(A) is possible. The political scientist claims that such bills do not allow for successful compromise, so it's highly likely that they usually don't get passed into law.

(B) is possible. Only bills that *are* of fundamental importance are presented as a problem. If most bills are *not* that important, then it is possible that most of them get compromises and get passed into law.

(D) is possible. There's no indication how many bills fit this description. It could be a few or it could be a lot. So, it's certainly possible for most bills to fit this description.

(E), like **(D)**, is possible. Again, there's no indication how many bills do or do not address important issues. Maybe it's 90% fundamentally important and 10% mildly important, or maybe it's 10% fundamentally important and 90% mildly important. So, it's possible for most bills to not be fundamentally important.

25. (E) Assumption (Necessary)

Step 1: Identify the Question Type

The question asks for an "assumption on which the argument depends," making this a Necessary Assumption question.

Step 2: Untangle the Stimulus

The author concludes ([*t*]*hus*) that used cars less than 10 years old (younger cars) are easier to sell than used cars 10 years old or older (older cars). The evidence is that it's easier to sell something when there's a higher demand for it. For junkyards, parts from younger cars are more easily resold than parts from older cars.

Step 3: Make a Prediction

The argument is based on the idea that car parts for younger cars are more in demand and are thus easier to sell. However, the conclusion is not about selling parts; it's about selling cars. For this argument to work, the author must assume that what's true for selling parts holds true for selling cars as a whole.

Step 4: Evaluate the Answer Choices

(E) must be true, suggesting that demand (and hence salability) for cars as a whole is equivalent to the demand for the parts. By the Denial Test, if that weren't true, then it would be possible for older cars to be easier to sell as a whole even if their individual parts are harder to sell. That would contradict the author, so it must be assumed that demand for whole cars and parts *are* equivalent.

(A) is Out of Scope. Even if there were other factors, demand could still be the most significant factor and the author's argument would be unaffected.

(B) is Extreme. Even if a few cars were sold elsewhere, that doesn't impact the difficultly level of reselling the car.

(C) is Extreme. The rule does not have to extend generally to all products. As long as it's true for cars, the argument is fine.

(D) is irrelevant. The argument is about the ease of selling, not the selling price or how such a price is derived.

Section II: Logic Games

Game 1: Instructional Film Presentations

Q#	Question Type	Correct	Difficulty
1	"If" / Must Be True	B	★
2	Must Be False (CANNOT Be True)	A	★
3	"If" / Could Be True EXCEPT	A	★
4	How Many	C	★★
5	"If" / Could Be True EXCEPT	B	★
6	"If" / Must Be False (CANNOT Be True)	B	★
7	Rule Substituion	C	★★

Game 2: Cafe Cosmopolitano Specials

Q#	Question Type	Correct	Difficulty
8	"If" / Could Be True	E	★★
9	Must Be False (CANNOT Be True)	D	★
10	Could Be True	E	★★★
11	Could Be True	A	★
12	Could Be True	B	★

Game 3: Investigators Interviewing Witnesses

Q#	Question Type	Correct	Difficulty
13	Acceptability	E	★
14	"If" / Must Be True	B	★
15	Could Be True	D	★★
16	"If" / Could Be True	A	★★★
17	Supply the If	B	★★
18	Could Be True EXCEPT	D	★★

Game 4: George, Rita, and Wendy's Student Presentations

Q#	Question Type	Correct	Difficulty
19	Acceptability	A	★
20	Must Be False (CANNOT Be True)	E	★★
21	"If" / Must Be True	D	★★
22	"If" / Could Be True	C	★★★
23	"If" / Could Be True	B	★★

Game 1: Instructional Film Presentations

Step 1: Overview
Situation: A company scheduling presentations of instructional films

Entities: Six films (*Goals, Management, Organization, Personnel, Sales, Utilization*) and two theaters (east and west)

Action: Distribution/Sequencing Hybrid. Determine the theater in which each film is presented (Distribution) and the order in which they are presented (Sequencing).

Limitations: There will be one presentation in each theater at each of three times (1:00, 2:00, and 3:00), for a total of six presentations. Each film will be presented exactly once.

Step 2: Sketch
List the films by initial. Set up a chart to assign the films, with one column for each theater. In each column, have three consecutive slots labeled 1, 2, and 3.

GMOPSU

	west	east
1	___	___
2	___	___
3	___	___

This allows the sketch to have the west on the left and east on the right (to mimic how west and east appear on a map). However, you could also set up three columns, one for each hour, putting the timeline from 1:00 to 3:00 to be seen from left to right, as might seem natural. Then, you have two rows, one for east and one for west. It's the exact same sketch, only rotated 90 degrees. Both would work fine.

Step 3: Rules
Rules 1 and 2 establish *Sales* and *Utilization* in the west and east theater, respectively. The times are unknown, so just draw "S" next to the west column and "U" next to the east column.

Rule 3 presents some loose sequencing: *Management* must be presented at some time before both *Organization* and *Personnel*. Note that this does not mean that *Management* must be presented at 1:00. It's also possible that *Management* is presented at 2:00 if both *Organization* and *Personnel* are presented at 3:00. So, for now, draw this rule in shorthand.

Rule 4 presents another loose relationship: *Utilization* must be presented before *Goals*.

U
|
G

Step 4: Deductions
The only duplicated entity is *Utilization*, which must be presented in the east theater (Rule 2) and at some point before *Goals* (Rule 4). That limits *Utilization* to 1:00 or 2:00, but *Utilization* only directly affects *Goals*. By Rule 3, *Management* is also limited to 1:00 or 2:00, but directly affects two other films. And placing *Management* at 2:00 leads to some significant deductions. Thus, Limited Options are warranted.

In Option I, *Management* will be presented at 1:00, although it could be in either theater. *Organization* and *Personnel* will each be presented at 2:00 or 3:00. They could be at the same time as each other or not. By Rule 4, *Utilization* has to be before *Goals*, so *Utilization* cannot be at 3:00 and, more importantly, *Goals* cannot be at 1:00. Along with *Management*, the other 1:00 film could only be *Utilization* or *Sales*.

I) GMOPSU

	west	east	
1	___	___	M, U/S
2	___	___	
3	___	___	~U

In Option II, *Management* will be presented at 2:00, in either theater. That means *Organization* and *Personnel* will both be presented at 3:00, one in each theater. With 3:00 complete, that leaves room at 1:00 at 2:00. *Utilization* must be presented before *Goals*, so *Utilization* must be at 1:00 (and, by Rule 2, in the east theater) and *Goals* will be at 2:00 with *Management*, in either theater. That leaves *Sales* to occupy the 1:00 slot in the west theater.

II) GMOPSU

	west	east
1	S	U
2	G/M	M/G
3	O/P	P/O

Step 5: Questions

1. (B) "If" / Must Be True
For this question, *Personnel* will be presented at 2:00. By Rule 3, that means *Management* must be presented at 1:00. That makes **(B)** correct. The remaining choices are all possible but need not be true. Typically, a New-"If" would warrant a new

sketch. However, in this case, the immediate deduction from placing *Personnel* first is the correct answer, so a new sketch is not necessary.

2. (A) Must Be False (CANNOT Be True)

The correct answer to this question will be impossible. The four wrong choices will be possible, if not definitely true.

Management must be presented before *Organization* and *Personnel*, which means *Management* can be presented at 2:00 at the latest. For *Goals* to be presented earlier, it would have to be presented at 1:00, but that would leave no room for *Utilization* before it, violating Rule 4. That makes **(A)** impossible and thus the correct answer. The remaining choices need not be true, but are all possible.

3. (A) "If" / Could Be True EXCEPT

For this question, *Goals* is presented at 3:00 in the east theater; that puts you in Option I. In that case, there's no room for both *Organization* and *Personnel* at 3:00, so one of them must be at 2:00, which forces *Management* to be presented at 1:00. With *Management* at 1:00, it cannot be presented at 2:00 in either theater, making **(A)** the correct answer.

4. (C) How Many

The correct answer to this question will be the number of films that could occupy a 3:00 slot in either theater. By Rule 3, *Management* must be earlier than other films, so *Management* cannot be at 3:00. Similarly, by Rule 4, *Utilization* cannot be at 3:00 because it must be presented before *Goals*. That leaves *Goals*, *Organization*, *Personnel*, and *Sales*, all of which could be presented at 3:00. That's a total of four films, making **(C)** correct. For further proof, Option II of the Limited Options confirms that *Organization* and *Personnel* can be presented at 3:00. And the following acceptable sketch confirms that *Goals* and *Sales* can be presented at 3:00.

	west	east
1	M	U
2	O/P	P/O
3	S	G

5. (B) "If" / Could Be True EXCEPT

For this question, *Utilization* will be presented at 2:00, and it must be in the east theater (Rule 2). That means *Goals* must be presented at 3:00 (Rule 4). In that case, there's no room for both *Organization* and *Personnel* at 3:00, so one of them must be at 2:00, which forces *Management* to be presented at 1:00. (This can be verified with Option I of the Limited Options.) With *Utilization* at 2:00 in the east theater, *Organization* or *Personnel* will be in the west theater at 2:00.

The other one will be presented at 3:00 along with *Goals*. That leaves *Sales* to be presented at 1:00 along with *Management*. *Sales* must be in the west theater (Rule 1), so *Management* will be in the east theater.

	west	east	
1	S	M	
2	O/P	U	
3	___	___	G, P/O

With that, *Management* cannot be presented at 2:00, making **(B)** the correct answer.

6. (B) "If" / Must Be False (CANNOT Be True)

For this question, *Management* is in the east theater at 2:00—that's Option II, which quickly leads to the correct answer. Without using the Limited Options though, if *Management* is in the east theater at 2:00, by Rule 3, *Organization* and *Personnel* are both presented at 3:00, one in each theater. With slots open in only 1:00 and 2:00, Rule 4 would require *Utilization* at 1:00 (in the east theater, by Rule 2) and *Goals* at 2:00 (in the west theater, as *Management* is in the east theater for this question). That leaves *Sales* for the west theater at 1:00.

	west	east
1	S	U
2	G	M
3	O/P	P/O

So, *Sales* is at 1:00, not 2:00, making **(B)** correct.

7. (C) Rule Substituion

The correct answer to this question will be a replacement for Rule 1 (*Sales* must be in the west theater) that will have the exact same effect. In other words, the correct answer must reestablish *Sales* in the west theater without adding any new restrictions.

The only other film that is assigned to a particular theater is *Utilization*, which must be in the east theater. If *Sales* is in a different theater than *Utilization*, then it would be back in the west theater, as desired. That's exactly what **(C)** offers, without adding any new, unnecessary restrictions.

For the record, *Sales* was never limited to any time frame, so **(A)** and **(E)** add unnecessary restrictions. And there was never any restriction between *Sales* and *Goals*, so it was never necessary for *Sales* to be at a different time or in a different theater from *Goals*. That eliminates **(B)** and **(D)**.

Game 2: Cafe Cosmopolitano Specials

Step 1: Overview
Situation: A restaurant offering daily specials

Entities: Five specials (gazpacho, linguini, nachos, pizza, quesadillas)

Action: Strict Sequencing. Determine the day on which each special is offered. As the days are consecutive (Monday through Saturday), the specials will be arranged in order.

Limitations: Exactly one special is offered each day. Note, though, that there are six days but only five specials. At least one special must be offered twice. And it's not until the first rule that each special is guaranteed to be offered. Without the first rule, it would have been possible, for example, to offer only gazpacho as the special throughout the week.

Step 2: Sketch
List the specials by initial and set up a horizontal set of six slots, labeled with each day, in order, from Monday through Saturday.

G L N P Q

___	___	___	___	___	___
Mo	Tu	We	Th	Fr	Sa

Step 3: Rules
Rules 1 and 2 establish the Numbers for the game. Every special must be used at least once. So, with five specials and six days, that means one special will be used twice. Furthermore, Rule 2 states that the one special that will be duplicated will not be offered on consecutive days. Shorthand notes for these two rules will suffice.

4 spec 1x
1 spec 2x
NEVER <u>X</u> <u>X</u>

Rule 3 limits gazpacho and nachos to one appearance each. Note this number restriction to the side, or draw a "1" above "G" and "N" in the entity list to keep track of the Numbers there.

Rule 4 creates a Block of Entities with quesadillas immediately before gazpacho whenever gazpacho is offered. It's important to note that quesadillas may be offered twice. If that happens, it will only be before gazpacho once. So, the block of quesadillas and gazpacho will appear at some point, but there could be a second appearance of quesadillas without gazpacho.

G → <u>Q</u> <u>G</u>

Rule 5 establishes pizza on Thursday and also keeps pizza out of Saturday. Add "P" to Thursday and draw "~P" under Saturday.

Rule 6 prevents quesadillas from being offered on Friday. Draw "~Q" under Friday.

Step 4: Deductions
Gazpacho and quesadillas are both duplicated in the rules, and they are the most significant entities of the game. Gazpacho will only be offered once, and it will be immediately preceded by quesadillas. Because of that, gazpacho cannot be offered on Monday. Thursday is occupied by pizza, which not only prevents gazpacho from being offered on Thursday, but also prevents gazpacho from being offered on Friday because there'd be no space before it for quesadillas. And finally, gazpacho cannot be offered on Saturday because Rule 6 prevents quesadillas from being offered on Friday. So, gazpacho can only be offered on Tuesday or Wednesday. Drawing out Limited Options will result in two sketches with Established Entities on half the days in each sketch.

In Option I, gazpacho will be offered on Tuesday, which means quesadillas will be offered on Monday. Nachos and linguini will each be offered on any one of the remaining days. Then there will be one duplicated special. It cannot be gazpacho or nachos (Rule 3). It also cannot be pizza, which cannot be on Saturday and cannot be on Wednesday or Friday because that would put the same special on consecutive days, violating Rule 2. Thus, either quesadillas or linguini will be duplicated on whichever day remains open.

I)

N, L, L/Q

Q	G	___	P	___	___
Mo	Tu	We	Th	Fr	Sa
		~P		~Q	~P
					~P

In Option II, gazpacho will be offered on Wednesday, which means quesadillas will be offered on Tuesday. Nachos and linguini will each be offered on any of the remaining days. Again, one special will be duplicated. It cannot be gazpacho or nachos (Rule 3), but it could be any of the remaining specials (linguini, pizza, or quesadillas). If pizza is duplicated, it cannot be on Friday (Rule 2) or Saturday (Rule 5). And if quesadillas are duplicated, it won't happen on Monday (Rule 2) or Friday (Rule 6).

II)   N, L, L/P/Q

	Q	G	P		
Mo	Tu	We	Th	Fr	Sa
~Q				~Q	~P
				~P	

Step 5: Questions

8. (E) "If" / Could Be True

For this question, linguini will be offered immediately before pizza. Pizza is already offered on Thursday, but could be offered twice. If it was, it could not be offered again on Saturday (Rule 5), nor could it be offered on Wednesday or Friday (Rule 2). Pizza cannot be offered on Tuesday without preventing the placement of the quesadillas and gazpacho block required by Rule 4. And having pizza on Monday would leave no room for linguini before it. So, the only days to have a block of linguini and pizza are Wednesday and Thursday. Quesadillas cannot be offered on Friday (Rule 6), so the only days to have the block of quesadillas and gazpacho are Monday and Tuesday.

$$N$$

Q	G	L	P		
Mo	Tu	We	Th	Fr	Sa

With that, all of the answer choices are false except for **(E)**, which could be true if linguini is the one special offered twice and nachos are offered on Saturday.

9. (D) Must Be False (CANNOT Be True)

The correct answer will be a day on which it is impossible to offer linguini. The remaining choices will list days that linguini could be offered. Linguini is a Floater and could seemingly be offered on any day. However, Thursday is already occupied by pizza. And gazpacho must be preceded immediately by quesadillas. Because quesadillas cannot be on Friday, the only days to place the block of quesadillas and gazpacho are Monday and Tuesday, or Tuesday and Wednesday (as drawn in the Limited Options). Either way, quesadillas or gazpacho must be on Tuesday, so linguini cannot be offered that day. That makes **(D)** correct.

10. (E) Could Be True

The correct answer will be the only one that could be true. The remaining choices must all be false.

Gazpacho cannot be offered on Monday because there would be no earlier day for quesadillas, violating Rule 4. That eliminates **(A)**. Per the Limited Options, only quesadillas or gazpacho could be on Tuesday, not nachos. That eliminates **(B)**. Pizza is offered on Thursday, so cannot be offered on Wednesday without violating Rule 2. That eliminates **(C)**. And gazpacho cannot be offered on Friday because pizza is on Thursday, which would make it impossible to follow Rule 4. That eliminates **(D)**, leaving **(E)** as the correct answer. Remember that quesadillas will be offered immediately before gazpacho once, but could be offered a second time—in this instance on Saturday.

11. (A) Could Be True

The correct answer will be a day on which pizza could be offered. The remaining choices will list days on which pizza could not be offered. By Rule 5, pizza cannot be offered on Saturday, so that eliminates **(E)**. Pizza is offered on Thursday, so it cannot be offered on Wednesday or Friday without violating Rule 2. That eliminates **(C)** and **(D)**. And as shown by the Limited Options, either gazpacho or quesadillas must be offered on Tuesday, so pizza cannot be offered that day. That eliminates **(B)**, leaving **(A)** as the correct answer.

12. (B) Could Be True

The correct answer will list a day on which gazpacho could be offered. The other choices will list days on which gazpacho cannot be offered.

The Limited Options were set up on the basis that gazpacho can only be offered on Tuesday or Wednesday. That makes **(B)** the correct answer. To recap: Gazpacho must be preceded by quesadillas, which eliminates Monday and thus **(A)**. Pizza is already on Thursday, which eliminates **(C)**. With pizza on Thursday, quesadillas cannot be offered then, so no gazpacho on Friday, eliminating **(D)**. And quesadillas are not offered on Friday (Rule 6), so gazpacho cannot be offered on Saturday. That eliminates **(E)**.

Game 3: Investigators Interviewing Witnesses

Step 1: Overview
Situation: Investigators interviewing witnesses at a prosecutor's office

Entities: Four witnesses (Farrell, Greer, Hong, Ikaba) and three investigators (Qin, Rivera, Shaw)

Action: Sequencing/Matching Hybrid. Determine the order in which the witnesses are interviewed (Sequencing), and then assign an investigator to each witness (Matching). Some may want to label this game just a Strict Sequencing game of two sequences (determine the order for both the witnesses and the investigators). Ultimately, it's not significant how the game is construed. No points are awarded on Test Day for proper classification. What's more important is that either of these designations would lead to the same sketch and application of the rules.

Limitations: Each witness will be interviewed once, one per day. Exactly one investigator will interview each witness, and each investigator must interview at least one witness. Note that there are only three investigators, so one will have to interview two witnesses.

Step 2: Sketch
Set up two rows of four slots, numbered 1 through 4. In the top row, order the witnesses (listed by initial). In the bottom row, assign the investigators (listed by initial). Use a different style for each group of people (e.g., uppercase vs. lowercase) to keep them separate when writing out rules.

$$
\begin{array}{cccc}
1 & 2 & 3 & 4 \\
\_\_ & \_\_ & \_\_ & \_\_ \quad FGHI \\
\_\_ & \_\_ & \_\_ & \_\_ \quad qrs
\end{array}
$$

Similarly, you could draw one set of slots and put the witness on top and the investigator on the bottom. Or, you can combine both into one slot using an uppercase letter for the witness and a subscript lowercase letter for the investigator (e.g., F_q). For these Explanations, two sets of slots will be used.

Step 3: Rules
Rule 1 dictates that Greer and Hong have the same investigator. For now, make a note of this to the side.

$$
\boxed{\begin{array}{cc} G & H \\ x & x \end{array}}
$$
$$
\underset{same}{\nwarrow \nearrow}
$$

Rule 2 prevents Greer and Ikaba from being interviewed consecutively, in either order.

Rule 3 establishes that Qin is interviewed by Farrell.

Rule 4 establishes Rivera as the investigator for the third witness. Add "r" to the appropriate space under day 3.

Step 4: Deductions
By Rule 1, the same investigator will interview Greer and Hong. It cannot be Qin, who already interviews Farrell (Rule 3). Otherwise, Qin would interview three witnesses, leaving only one witness (Ikaba) for two investigators. So, Greer and Hong could only be interviewed by Rivera or Shaw. Whichever one doesn't interview Greer and Hong will be left to interview Ikaba. That creates two options in which all of the witnesses are paired up with an investigator. And with Rivera established on day 3, Limited Options are worth considering.

In Option I, Qin interviews Farrell, Rivera interviews Greer and Hong, and Shaw interviews Ikaba. That means either Greer or Hong will be interviewed third by Rivera.

$$
\begin{array}{l}
\text{I)} \quad
\begin{array}{cccc}
1 & 2 & 3 & 4 \\
\_\_ & \_\_ & G/H & \_\_ \\
\_\_ & \_\_ & r & \_\_
\end{array}
\quad
\boxed{\begin{array}{c} F \\ q \end{array}}
\boxed{\begin{array}{c} H/G \\ r \end{array}}
\boxed{\begin{array}{c} I \\ s \end{array}}
\end{array}
$$

In Option II, Qin interviews Farrell, Rivera interviews Ikaba, and Shaw interviews Greer and Hong. That means Ikaba is interviewed by Rivera third. Because Greer and Ikaba cannot be interviewed consecutively, Greer will be interviewed by Shaw first. That leaves Farrell and Hong to be interviewed second and fourth, in either order.

$$
\begin{array}{l}
\text{II)} \quad
\begin{array}{cccc}
1 & 2 & 3 & 4 \\
G & \_\_ & I & \_\_ \\
s & \_\_ & r & \_\_
\end{array}
\quad
\boxed{\begin{array}{c} F \\ q \end{array}}
\boxed{\begin{array}{c} H \\ s \end{array}}
\end{array}
$$

Step 5: Questions

13. (E) Acceptability
As with any Acceptability question, go through the rules one at a time to eliminate choices that violate the rules.

(C) violates Rule 1 by having different investigators interview Greer and Hong. **(B)** violates Rule 2 by having Ikaba interviewed immediately before Greer. **(A)** violates Rule 3 by having Shaw, not Qin, interview Farrell. **(D)** violates Rule 4 by having Qin, not Rivera, conduct the third interview. That leaves **(E)** as the correct answer.

14. (B) "If" / Must Be True

For this question, Rivera interviews Ikaba. With Qin interviewing Farrell, that leaves Shaw to interview Greer and Hong. Rivera will interview Ikaba third (Rule 4), which means Greer must be interviewed first (Rule 2). Farrell and Hong will be interviewed second and fourth, in either order. (This is the basis of Option II in Limited Options.)

II) 1   2   3   4
G __ I __ | F | H |
s __ r __ | q | s |

With Greer first, **(B)** is correct. The remaining choices are false or need not be true.

15. (D) Could Be True

The correct answer will be the only one that could be true. The remaining choices must be false.

Qin can only conduct one interview, Farrell's, because the investigator who conducts two interviews will interview Greer and Hong. That eliminates **(A)** and **(B)**.

Rivera already conducts the third interview. If Rivera conducted the second and the fourth, that would be three interviews. That would only leave one interview for the remaining two investigators. That eliminates **(C)**.

If Shaw interviews two witnesses, it must be Greer and Hong—as seen in Option II. In that scenario, Qin interviews Farrell, leaving Rivera to interview Ikaba. Rivera interviews the third witness, so that would be Ikaba's interview. Greer would then have to be interviewed by Shaw first (Rule 2). Hong could be interviewed second or fourth, so Shaw could interview witnesses first and second or first and fourth. Only **(D)** is possible, making it the correct answer.

16. (A) "If" / Could Be True

For this question, Shaw conducts the fourth interview. With Qin interviewing Farrell, Shaw could interview Greer and Hong, or Shaw could interview Ikaba. Draw out both options (which would use the same basis as the Limited Options).

If Shaw interviews Greer and Hong, Rivera is left to interview Ikaba, which would happen third (Rule 4). That would force Greer to be interviewed by Shaw first (Rule 2). For Shaw to conduct the fourth interview, it must be with Hong, leaving Qin to interview Farrell second.

1   2   3   4
G   F   I   H
s   q   r   s

If Shaw interviews Ikaba, that will happen fourth for this question. Rivera interviews Greer and Hong, but cannot interview Greer third (Rule 2). So, Rivera interviews Hong third, leaving Greer and Farrell to be interviewed first and second, in either order.

1   2   3   4
__ __ H   I | F | G |
__ __ r   s | q | r |

That allows Farrell to be interviewed first, making **(A)** the correct answer. None of the remaining choices is possible in either outcome.

17. (B) Supply the If

The correct answer will be the one that, if true, would force Farrell to be interviewed fourth. The remaining choices would still allow Farrell to be interviewed at another time.

If Greer is interviewed first, then Ikaba could be interviewed third or fourth. Because Ikaba could be interviewed fourth, Farrell need not be. That eliminates **(A)**.

If Hong is interviewed second, that limits the placement of Greer and Ikaba. They must be split up, so one of them is interviewed first. That means Farrell can only be interviewed third or fourth. However, Farrell is interviewed by Qin, not Rivera, so Farrell would have to be interviewed fourth in this case.

1   2   3   4
__ H   __ F
__ __ r   q

That makes **(B)** correct. For the record:

If Hong is interviewed third, then Greer and Ikaba still need to be split. They can't be first and second, so one of them would have to be fourth, preventing Farrell from being fourth. That eliminates **(C)**.

If Ikaba is first, Greer could be third or fourth. Because Greer could be fourth, Farrell need not be. That eliminates **(D)**.

If Ikaba is second, Greer would have to be fourth, not Farrell. That eliminates **(E)**.

18. (D) Could Be True EXCEPT

The four wrong choices all could be true. That means the correct answer must be false.

The quickest way to answer this question is to refer back to the sketches for the fourth question of this game. Between the two outcomes, **(A)**, **(B)**, **(C)**, and **(E)** are all seen as possible. Thus, they can all be eliminated, leaving **(D)** as the correct answer. For the record:

If Hong and Farrell were first and second, that would force Greer and Ikaba to be consecutive, violating Rule 2. The same would happen if Hong and Farrell were third and fourth. To split Greer and Ikaba, Hong and Farrell would have to be second and third. However, having Hong immediately before Farrell would put Farrell third, which violates Rule 4 because Farrell must be interviewed by Qin. So, it is indeed impossible to have Hong immediately before Farrell.

Game 4: George, Rita, and Wendy's Student Presentations

Step 1: Overview

Situation: A teacher assigning students presentations on three rather cerebral and somewhat nefarious subjects

Entities: Three students (George, Rita, Wendy) and three presentation subjects (Machiavellianism, jitsuaku, Shakespeare's villains)

Action: Matching. Determine which subjects are assigned to each student.

Limitations: Each student will be assigned at least one subject, and each subject is assigned to at least one student.

Step 2: Sketch

Because the subjects are being assigned, it makes sense to set up a column for each student. Each column will get one slot to start. List the subjects by initial to the side.

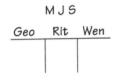

It's also possible to set up a chart with three columns, one for each subject. The logic would apply effectively either way.

Step 3: Rules

Rules 1, 2, and 3 all provide Formal Logic. Translate each rule and its contrapositive, and write them all to the side. First, if George presents on jitsuaku, then so does Rita. By contrapositive, if Rita does not present on jitsuaku, then neither does George.

$$\frac{Geo}{J} \rightarrow \frac{Rit}{J}$$

$$\sim\frac{Rit}{J} \rightarrow \sim\frac{Geo}{J}$$

Second, if Rita presents on Shakespeare's villains, then Wendy does not. By contrapositive, if Wendy does present on Shakespeare's villains, then Rita does not.

$$\frac{Rit}{S} \rightarrow \sim\frac{Wen}{S}$$

$$\frac{Wen}{S} \rightarrow \sim\frac{Rit}{S}$$

Third, if anyone presents on Machiavellianism, then that person also presents on Shakespeare's villains. By contrapositive, if anyone does not present on Shakespeare's villains, then that person does not present on Machiavellianism.

$$M \rightarrow S$$
$$\sim S \rightarrow \sim M$$

Step 4: Deductions

Because each rule involves Formal Logic, there are no concrete deductions to be made. Nothing can happen for certain unless a condition is triggered. However, each rule has an implication that is worth considering before moving on to the questions.

By the contrapositive of Rule 1, if Rita does not present on jitsuaku, then neither does George. However, somebody has to be present on jitsuaku. In that case, it would have to be Wendy. So, if Rita does not present on jitsuaku, then Wendy does. In other words, either Rita or Wendy must present on jitsuaku, perhaps both.

By Rule 2, assigning Shakespeare's villains to Rita prevents it from being assigned to Wendy. In short, that means Rita and Wendy can't both present on Shakespeare's villains. Only one of them can, and perhaps George. It's also possible that neither one presents on it, and only George does.

By the contrapositive of Rule 3, if someone does not present on Shakespeare's villains, that person does not present on Machiavellianism. However, everyone has to present on something. In that case, the person would have to present on jitsuaku. So, if someone does not present on Shakespeare's villains, that person must present on jitsuaku. In other words, each person must present on Shakespeare's villains or jitsuaku, or perhaps both.

Step 5: Questions

19. (A) Acceptability

As with any Acceptability question, go through the rules one at a time and eliminate answers that violate those rules.

(D) violates Rule 1 by assigning jitsuaku to George but not Rita. **(B)** violates Rule 2 by assigning Shakespeare's villains to Rita and also to Wendy. **(C)** violates Rule 3 by assigning Wendy Machiavellianism but not Shakespeare's villains. **(E)** also violates Rule 3 by assigning Rita Machiavellianism but not Shakespeare's villains. That leaves **(A)** as the correct answer. (Note that this does not violate Rule 3. It's okay for Wendy to be assigned Shakespeare's villains without being assigned Machiavellianism. It's the other way around that would be unacceptable.)

20. (E) Must Be False (CANNOT Be True)

The correct answer will be an unacceptable list of students assigned Machiavellianism (i.e., must be false). The remaining choices could all be acceptable assignments.

By Rule 3, any student who presents on Machiavellianism also presents on Shakespeare's villains. That means each choice here lists people who present on both Machiavellianism and Shakespeare's villains. However, by Rule 2, if Rita presents on Shakespeare's villains, Wendy cannot. Thus, it's impossible for both Rita and Wendy to present on Machiavellianism as it would mean they'd both present on Shakespeare's villains, violating Rule 2. That means **(E)** is not possible and thus the correct answer.

21. (D) "If" / Must Be True

For this question, Wendy presents on exactly two subjects, which means she won't present on the third. If she didn't present on Shakespeare's villains, then she couldn't present on Machiavellianism (Rule 3). That would leave just one subject (jitsuaku), which is not acceptable here. So, she must present on Shakespeare's villains. The second subject could be either Machiavellianism or jitsuaku. Don't misinterpret Rule 3 here. She can't present on Machiavellianism without Shakespeare's villains, but it's okay to present on Shakespeare's villains and not Machiavellianism.

In addition, because Wendy presents on Shakespeare's villains, Rita cannot (Rule 2). Because Rita can't present on Shakespeare's villains, she can't present on Machiavellianism either (Rule 3), and thus must present on jitsuaku.

Geo	Rit	Wen
	J	S
		J/M
	~S	
	~M	

That makes **(D)** correct. Note that, by Rule 1, it is acceptable for George to also present on jitsuaku, but he doesn't have to.

22. (C) "If" / Could Be True

For this question, George presents on one subject: jitsuaku. By Rule 1, that means Rita does, too. Somebody still has to present on Machiavellianism, and that person will also present on Shakespeare's villains. George is done, and Rita and Wendy cannot both present on Shakespeare's villains (Rule 2). So, only one of Rita and Wendy will get that assignment. Test both options.

If Rita presents on Machiavellianism, then she presents on Shakespeare's villains, and thus all three subjects. By Rule 2, Wendy can no longer present on Shakespeare's villains, and thus cannot present on Machiavellianism. That leaves her with only jitsuaku.

Geo	Rit	Wen
J	J	J
	M	
	S	

If Wendy presents on Machiavellianism, then she presents on Shakespeare's villains (Rule 3). By Rule 2, Rita can no longer present on Shakespeare's villains, and thus cannot present on Machiavellianism. That leaves her with jitsuaku only. Wendy can still present on jitsuaku, but need not.

Geo	Rit	Wen
J	J	M
		S
	~S	
	~M	

With that, only **(C)** is possible (in the first outcome), making it correct.

23. (B) "If" / Could Be True

For this question, Wendy presents on jitsuaku and Shakespeare's villains, but not Machiavellianism. Because Wendy presents on Shakespeare's villains, Rita cannot (Rule 2), and thus cannot present on Machiavellianism (Rule 3). That leaves Rita with only jitsuaku. By Rule 1, it is possible for George to now also present on jitsuaku, but he need not. However, because neither Rita nor Wendy present on Machiavellianism, George must, which then means he must also present on Shakespeare's villains (Rule 3).

Geo	Rit	Wen
M	J	J
S		S
	~S	~M
	~M	

With that, only **(B)** could be true and is thus correct.

Section III: Reading Comprehension
Passage 1: The Economics of Forest Preservation

Q#	Question Type	Correct	Difficulty
1	Global	A	★
2	Inference	C	★
3	Detail	C	★
4	Logic Reasoning (Parallel Reasoning)	E	★★
5	Global	E	★
6	Inference	A	★
7	Inference	B	★★★★

Passage 2: Indigenous Language Preservation Using Radio

Q#	Question Type	Correct	Difficulty
8	Global	B	★★
9	Inference	B	★
10	Logic Function	C	★
11	Inference	A	★★
12	Detail	A	★
13	Logic Reasoning (Parallel Reasoning)	D	★★

Passage 3: The Need for Judicial Candor

Q#	Question Type	Correct	Difficulty
14	Global	B	★★
15	Inference	B	★★
16	Logic Reasoning (Point at Issue)	C	★★★
17	Logic Reasoning (Principle)	B	★★
18	Inference	D	★★★★
19	Detail	E	★★★
20	Logic Reasoning (Point at Issue)	E	★★★
21	Logic Reasoning (Parallel Reasoning)	C	★★★★

Passage 4: The Fall of Grand Theories

Q#	Question Type	Correct	Difficulty
22	Global	D	★★
23	Inference (Author's Attitude)	C	★★
24	Global	C	★★★
25	Logic Function	B	★★★
26	Detail	D	★★★
27	Inference	E	★★★★

Passage 1: The Economics of Forest Preservation

Step 1: Read the Passage Strategically
Sample Roadmap

Line #	Keyword/phrase	¶ Margin notes
1	most valuable	
2	both	
6	However; if	Policy makers need info on forests
10	should	
12	Two	
13	one	2 claims
14	the other	
15	merit special scrutiny	
16	Some consider	
21	But	
21–22	largely a myth	Forests do not produce a net gain in oxygen
23	but	
25	therefore	
27	Another claim	
30	For one thing	Biodiversity for medicine
34	crucial	
35	But even if	
37–38	widely held by some	Biodiversity for moral reasons
38	moral imperative	
41	Actually	
42	not	
43	claimed	
44	however	
45	some people are highly critical	Plantations have less biodiversity
46	significantly	
47	However; since	
51	In addition	but they take econ pressure off true forests
52	overstated	
55	just	Plantations a small percentage

Discussion

The author starts off by noting how *valuable* forests (Topic) are, both economically and ecologically. After some facts illustrating the value of forests, the author raises a concern. To make sound policies on forest preservation, policy makers need a "comprehensive understanding" of arguments regarding the economic use of forests. And the author wants to focus on two claims in particular: 1) Forests renew oxygen, and 2) forests preserve biodiversity. As can be expected, the following paragraphs go into detail about these claims, making the discussion of these arguments the Scope of the passage.

The claim about oxygen renewal is discussed in the second paragraph. Some people argue that trees produce so much oxygen that there would be no oxygen without forests. *But*, the author argues this is a myth. Yes, trees produce oxygen, but they absorb just as much oxygen when decomposing. *Therefore*, everything cancels out.

The third paragraph discusses the second claim, with people arguing that forests are home to plants that can provide valuable medical resources. And even without the medical argument, forests house diverse animal species, and people claim that we're morally obligated to conserve forests to protect these animals.

In the final paragraph, the author argues that deforestation is not happening as quickly as some people believe. The author introduces additional concerns about commercial plantations in forests, but swiftly provides more counterarguments to those concerns: 1) Those plantations produce wood and wood pulp so that we don't have to eliminate true forests, thus allowing such forests to continue supporting biodiversity, and 2) plantations make up a very small percentage of forest area.

The Purpose of the passage is to present the arguments and counterarguments regarding forest preservation. And this serves to support the Main Idea presented in the first paragraph: Policy makers need to consider all sides of such arguments if they're to make sound policy decisions.

1. (A) Global

Step 2: Identify the Question Type
The question asks for the "main point of the passage," making this a Global question.

Step 3: Research the Relevant Text
There's no need to go back into the passage. Refer to the Main Idea as predicted after reading the passage.

Step 4: Make a Prediction
The Main Idea is that, to make sound policy decisions regarding forest use and preservation, policy makers need to thoroughly understand the relevant arguments.

Step 5: Evaluate the Answer Choices
(A) is a concise summary of the author's point.

(B) is too narrow, focusing only on the biodiversity issue. Further, there's no support for the opinions cited here (dangers are *insignificant*; regulation attempts are *ill-considered*).

(C) refers to statistics from the last paragraph, but completely misses the point about how such information should be considered when making policy decisions.

(D) is too narrow, focusing on (and distorting) the views presented in the third paragraph. This ignores the author's counterarguments and how they relate to policy decisions.

(E) is too narrow and goes Out of Scope. Plantations are just one issue raised in the last paragraph. And the author never discusses the potential effectiveness of regulations on them.

2. (C) Inference

Step 2: Identify the Question Type
The question asks for something that "can be inferred from the passage," making this an Inference question.

Step 3: Research the Relevant Text
Specifically, the question asks for something "scientists believe" about "rain-forest plants," phrases found in line 31 in the third paragraph.

Step 4: Make a Prediction
Lines 30–35 describe the belief that these plants have "unique disease-fighting properties" and can "offer clues, as well as basic materials, for research on new medications."

Step 5: Evaluate the Answer Choices
(C) directly addresses the scientists' beliefs.

(A) is an Extreme Distortion. The scientists say *some* rain-forest plant species have such properties, but never say this is limited to a "tiny proportion" of such plants.

(B) is Out of Scope. The plants are said to have "disease-fighting properties," but it's never said what kinds of diseases, let alone whether they're "endemic to tropical regions."

(D) is a Faulty Use of Detail. Absorption of carbon dioxide and oxygen are discussed in the second paragraph, with no relation to the scientists' view on rain-forest plants.

(E) is Extreme and unsupported. The scientists are probably eager to preserve such plants, but there is no evidence that these plants are "almost completely extinct."

3. (C) Detail

Step 2: Identify the Question Type
The correct answer will be a question that is directly answered by a detail in the passage.

Step 3: Research the Relevant Text
There are no Content Clues or line references, so the entire text is relevant.

Step 4: Make a Prediction
With no research clues, a prediction is not possible. Instead, go through the choices one at a time, only doing research when necessary to ensure the question in the correct choice is answered.

Step 5: Evaluate the Answer Choices
(C) is answered in line 22: Plants produce oxygen by photosynthesis.

(A) is not answered. The Brazilian Amazon rain forest is mentioned in line 17, but there are no statistics regarding its size with respect to the world's rain forests.

(B) is not answered. It is mentioned that plantations produce wood and wood pulp (lines 48–49), but that is not necessarily all plantations produce. And no exact count is provided. In lines 3–4, it is said "over 5,000 commercial products" come from forests—however, that is from all forests, and is not limited to just "commercial plantations."

(D) is Out of Scope. The passage concerns policy decisions in general, but the author makes no mention of specific measures that can be taken.

(E) is Out of Scope. No comparison is made between rain-forest trees and either other types of vegetation in rain forests or vegetation in other environments.

4. (E) Logic Reasoning (Parallel Reasoning)
Step 2: Identify the Question Type
The correct choice will be a situation "most analogous" to one described in the passage. That makes this a Parallel Reasoning question like those found in Logical Reasoning.

Step 3: Research the Relevant Text
The question directly addresses the relationship described in lines 22–26.

Step 4: Make a Prediction
The relationship described in lines 22–26 is one of zero sum. Oxygen is produced through one process, but an equal amount is consumed through another process. Overall, no gain and no loss. The correct answer will describe a similar situation in which gains and losses are completely balanced out.

Step 5: Evaluate the Answer Choices
(E) is a perfect match. The amount of water that is lost (evaporates in hot weather) is completely balanced out when that same water is regained (returns as rain or snow). Overall, no gain and no loss.

(A) is close, as it describes a gain (increase in purchasing power due to increased pay) being counterbalanced by a loss (decrease in purchasing power due to inflation). However, the

gain here is only said to be "partially eroded." So, it's not a complete zero sum. There's still an overall gain.

(B) does not match. There is no gain being counterbalanced by a loss.

(C) does not match. If anything, it might be implied that expended energy costs money, and that is counterbalanced by cash returns. However, it's not zero sum. The cash return "more than pays" for the expended energy costs. There's an overall gain.

(D) does not match. This describes how one gain can lead to another gain. There is no counterbalance of any loss.

5. (E) Global
Step 2: Identify the Question Type
The question asks what the author is "primarily concerned with," making this a Global question.

Step 3: Research the Relevant Text
There's no need to go back into the passage. The primary concern can be predicted using the Scope, as determined while reading the passage.

Step 4: Make a Prediction
The author is primarily concerned with the arguments and counterarguments regarding issues relevant to forest preservation policies.

Step 5: Evaluate the Answer Choices
(E) matches the author's focus.

(A) is a Distortion. The author wants policy makers to be informed, but the author is not personally making any policy proposals.

(B) is Out of Scope. The author offers no "scientific solutions" to any problems.

(C) is Out of Scope. Scientists may be interested in exploiting plants for medical purposes, but the author doesn't offer any new ways to do so. Besides, that's not the author's main concern.

(D) is a Distortion. The author just wants policy makers to be more informed. The author is not choosing sides or drumming up support for forest preservation.

6. (A) Inference
Step 2: Identify the Question Type
The question asks for a statement "most consistent with the views of the author." That makes this is an Inference question; the correct answer will be supported by the text from the passage but not directly stated.

Step 3: Research the Relevant Text
The author expresses views about commercial plantations in the fourth paragraph.

Step 4: Make a Prediction

According to the passage, some people are critical because plantations contain fewer plant and animal species than natural forests (lines 45–47). However, the author responds to that by arguing that plantations actually reduce pressure on natural forests, allowing those forests to better support biodiversity. So, the correct answer should indicate that the critics are (literally) not seeing the forest for the trees, i.e., they're not considering the complete picture about the effect of plantations on forest biodiversity.

Step 5: Evaluate the Answer Choices

(A) is correct. Critics only point to the lack of plant and animal diversity within the commercial plantations, and they don't see how such plantations actually help the supportive nature of true, noncommercial forests.

(B) is a Faulty Use of Detail. The scientists concerned with medical potential are described in the third paragraph, completely separate from those concerned with plantations.

(C) is a Faulty Use of Detail. Photosynthesis and biomass are concepts that address the oxygen production argument in the second paragraph, not the plantation argument.

(D) is a 180. The author's counterarguments in lines 47–56 indicate that critics are overlooking details.

(E) is a 180 and Out of Scope. The author's counterarguments in the fourth paragraph are meant to suggest that critics do not understand the big picture. Besides, the author is focused on forests in this passage, not overall global environmental issues.

7. (B) Inference

Step 2: Identify the Question Type

The correct answer will be "strongly supported by the information" provided, making this an Inference question.

Step 3: Research the Relevant Text

There are no Content Clues and no line references, so the entire text is relevant.

Step 4: Make a Prediction

With no reference point, there are too many possible inferences to make a reliable prediction. Instead, go through the choices one at a time, and use clues in the choices to do any necessary research.

Step 5: Evaluate the Answer Choices

(B) is supported, even if loosely. According to the first paragraph, forests are valuable because they help "prevent soil erosion that clogs rivers with silt." The implication is that, without forests, there would be more clogged rivers, which would undoubtedly affect water-based transportation.

(A) is not supported. Rain-forest plants are said to have "disease-fighting properties," but there's no indication that any of these diseases affect both plants and humans.

(C) is likely a 180. According to the last sentence, commercial plantations make up only 3% of the world's forest area. That leaves 97% for other forest types, so it's probable that other forest types are far more common.

(D) is not supported. Regarding biodiversity, no comparison is made between tropical rain forests and other forests.

(E) is Out of Scope. The plantations are said to produce wood and wood pulp, but there's no indication of where those products are used, be it in the same country or elsewhere.

Passage 2: Indigenous Language Preservation Using Radio

Step 1: Read the Passage Strategically
Sample Roadmap

Line #	Keyword/phrase	¶ Margin notes
6	due in large part; misguided	Dec. native lang due to gov't policies
8	mandated	
10	discouraged	
11	Yet; despite	
12	resurgence	Recent inc. native lang study
19	Because	
20	particularly effective	
23	In fact	Radio especially effective
27	also helped	
31	However	
32	could counter	Danger of Internet
35	considerable energy	
38	but	
39	not enough	Radio can help, but needs to tie to oral tradition
40	to be effective; countering	
41	deleterious	
42	should resonate	
44	noted	
47	but	
50	unengaging and distant	Lessons unengaging
52	By contrast; effective; should	Effective programming
57	success at revitalizing	
58	Similarly	

Discussion

The passage opens with statistics about indigenous languages in the United States (Topic). There are now far fewer languages than there were in the past, and more may be lost. According to the author, this is largely *due to* government policies that mandated the teaching of English to Native Americans. *Yet*, the author cites sources of a resurgence in studying and preserving such languages: college courses, video footage, and radio broadcasts.

In the second paragraph, the author focuses on radio broadcasts as an "effective tool for preserving" these languages, making this the Scope of the passage. The paragraph describes how the accessibility of radio has made it a source of promoting native languages and strengthening community ties.

However, the third paragraph raises a potential problem: the Internet, which generally requires users to focus on learning English instead. The author insists that radio could counter this, but it has to do so by tying in to oral traditions.

To emphasize this last point, in the fourth paragraph, the author cites a study showing how programming that resonates with oral tradition is common in communities where English is still secondary. In communities where English is now dominant, radio programming in the native language is merely educational and lacks a cultural context. The author concludes with suggestions for what effective programming should include, such as recordings of elders and traditional songs.

The author's Purpose is to describe how radio can help in preserving indigenous languages. The Main Idea is that if used properly, radio can be an effective tool for preserving languages and even counteract the negative influence of the Internet.

8. (B) Global

Step 2: Identify the Question Type
The question asks for the "main point of the passage," making this a Global question.

Step 3: Research the Relevant Text
There's no need to go back into the passage. Instead, consider the Main Idea derived while reading the passage.

Step 4: Make a Prediction
The Main Idea is that radio programming can be an effective tool for preserving indigenous languages.

Step 5: Evaluate the Answer Choices
(B) accurately captures the main point, even addressing the point from the third paragraph about how radio programming can counter the threat from the Internet.

(A) is Extreme and a Distortion. The author merely claims that the Internet *could* counter the influence of radio (lines 31–33),

not that it already has. Besides, the passage overall is focused on the potential benefit of radio, not the negative effect of the Internet.

(C) is Extreme. The author claims that radio can be effective in countering the effect of the Internet (lines 39–42), not that it is the *only* way to combat the Internet.

(D) is a Faulty Use of Detail. This focuses merely on the importance of cultural context without tying that to the primary scope of the passage: radio programming.

(E) makes an unsupported comparison of radio programming to "other approaches." And the idea of stimulating a rekindled interest among older people is mentioned briefly in lines 28–30, but that is not presented as the main point for why radio programming works.

9. (B) Inference

Step 2: Identify the Question Type
The question asks for something that the "passage most strongly suggests," making this an Inference question.

Step 3: Research the Relevant Text
The question asks for the type of radio programming that would lend itself to successful preservation. This is the author's focus from the end of the third paragraph through to the end.

Step 4: Make a Prediction
At the end of the third paragraph, the author suggests that successful programming should "resonate with the living oral traditions" of the community. Evidence in the fourth paragraph supports this, showing how unsuccessful programming is "unengaging and distant from the cultural contexts." So, programs that are less likely to be successful are ones that resist cultural context.

Step 5: Evaluate the Answer Choices
(B) is correct, as it is the only one to address the failure to connect language to the culture.

(A) is Out of Scope. The description (or lack thereof) of daily life is never suggested as a factor in a program's success.

(C) is Out of Scope. Economic circumstances are not presented as significant to a program's success.

(D) is a Distortion. The less successful programs do advocate the use of native languages, but they do so in the form of educational lessons. It's the lack of cultural context that causes them to fail.

(E) is a 180. The less successful programs do use academic methods. It's their reliance on such methods without a cultural context that makes them less successful.

10. (C) Logic Function

Step 2: Identify the Question Type
The question asks for the "primary purpose" of a particular claim, making this a Logic Function question.

Step 3: Research the Relevant Text
The author mentions native language curricula in the first paragraph (lines 13–15). However, Logic Function questions are all about context, so consult the margin notes to understand the broader purpose of the surrounding lines.

Step 4: Make a Prediction
The curricula is brought up as the author is discussing the "resurgence in native language study and preservation efforts." The increase in Native American language curricula is one of several examples (including film recordings and radio programming) used to illustrate this resurgence.

Step 5: Evaluate the Answer Choices
(C) is a match.

(A) is a Distortion. The author claims radio programming is "particularly effective" (line 20), but never goes so far as to suggest that it's any more or less effective than other methods, including a greater number of native language curricula.

(B) is a Distortion. The increase in curricula and the development of radio programming are discussed separately. There's no suggestion that either one is an effect of the other.

(D) is a Faulty Use of Detail. Sure, the scholars mentioned are promoting native languages and the government policies promoted English. However, while that difference can certainly be noted, that wasn't the author's intention. The author was trying to illustrate a resurgence in language preservation.

(E) is a Distortion. University curricula and radio programming are presented as separate entities. There is no suggestion that one had any effect on the other.

11. (A) Inference

Step 2: Identify the Question Type
The question asks for something with which the author is "most likely to agree," making this an Inference question.

Step 3: Research the Relevant Text
There are no research clues, so the entire passage is relevant.

Step 4: Make a Prediction
With no reference point, it's not possible to make a reliable prediction. Instead, go through the choices one at a time and only research what's necessary.

Step 5: Evaluate the Answer Choices
(A) is supported. The author laments the *misguided* attempts to mandate the teaching of English to Native Americans, which supports the desirability of preserving native

languages. And the author is frequently pushing the cultural and community-based components of radio programs as the key to successful preservation.

(B) is Extreme. While such cooperation can make radio programming effective, that's not to say that language preservation will absolutely fail without such cooperation.

(C) is Out of Scope. The author never mentions consensus among elders as a roadblock, let alone the *main* roadblock.

(D) is a Distortion. The key to success is focusing on cultural and community-based issues. There's no indication that technological and economic developments are relevant enough to matter.

(E) is Extreme. While native language curricula is presented as a sign of greater preservation, there's no suggestion that devoting even more resources (let alone *significantly* more) to such curricula is necessary.

12. (A) Detail

Step 2: Identify the Question Type
The question asks for something the passage directly states, making this a Detail question.

Step 3: Research the Relevant Text
The recent growth in the study of native languages is mentioned in the first paragraph. A good place to start is the line involving the "resurgence in native language study" (line 12).

Step 4: Make a Prediction
According to the author, the resurgence in studying native languages has been happening "despite the residual effects" of the efforts mentioned earlier in the paragraph, namely the "misguided U.S. government policies" that "mandated the teaching of English to all Native Americans."

Step 5: Evaluate the Answer Choices
(A) matches the text of the passage.

(B) is Out of Scope. There is no indication that government or university officials have changed their attitude.

(C) is Out of Scope. The author never mentions the potential "loss of scholarship."

(D) is a Distortion. The establishment of radio programming is indeed a sign of increased study and preservation efforts. However, there is no language in the passage to indicate radio programming has replaced other types of language transmission.

(E) is a 180. According to the passage, curricula is being developed by Native American scholars. There's no suggestion such scholars are lacking.

13. (D) Logic Reasoning (Parallel Reasoning)

Step 2: Identify the Question Type

The question asks for examples of what the author recommends. These will not be stated in the passage, but will be an inference based on the author's language. Further, the word EXCEPT indicates that four choices will be supported. The correct answer will not be a valid example.

Step 3: Research the Relevant Text

The question directly refers to the fourth paragraph, specifically the author's recommendations, which can be found in lines 52–62.

Step 4: Make a Prediction

In the fourth paragraph, the author recommends "recordings of elders . . . , word games . . . , and speeches by fluent speakers" (lines 53–55). The author also advocates for "integrating traditional songs" (line 59). Four answers will reflect these recommendations. The correct answer will be something unrelated.

Step 5: Evaluate the Answer Choices

(D) is correct. Such educational lessons are more in line with the less successful programs described in lines 47–52.

(A) is an example of "speeches by fluent speakers" (line 55).

(B) is an example of "integrating traditional songs into a presentation of a native language" (lines 59–60).

(C) is an example of "recordings of elders speaking the native language" (line 53–54).

(E) is an example of "speeches by fluent speakers" (line 55).

Passage 3: The Need for Judicial Candor

Step 1: Read the Passage Strategically
Sample Roadmap

Line #	Keyword/phrase	¶ Margin notes
Passage A		
3	argue	
4	ignores	Arguments against judicial sincerity
9	dangerously	
10	two ways	2 ways to defend sincerity
11	first	
15	justified	1) Prudential
16	Accordingly	
17	for example	
21	problem	
22	fails	But there is reason to be sincere even w/o good outcomes
26	merely; Rather	
28	second	2) Morality
30	appealing to; rather than	
Passage B		
34	vital	Pro-sincerity
35	But	
36	?	
36–37	reasons to think so	
39–40	greatly diluted	
40	since	Without sincerity much less constraint
44	essential prerequisite	
48	Moreover	Detecting lack of sincerity = inc. cynicism
52	unshakable; ?	
54	?	Not absolutely required
54–55	Probably not	
55	But	
56	must	but cost-benefit typically favors candor
60	strong presumption in favor	

Discussion

The author of passage A begins with the opinion of "some legal theorists." When a passage opens with such an opinion, it usually introduces the Topic and Scope of the passage. Further, you can expect the author or somebody else to reject that opinion, and that will usually provide insight into the Purpose and Main Idea of the passage.

Here, the entire first paragraph is devoted to the theorists' opinion. They argue that judges do not have to believe what they say when rendering their opinions. In other words, they shouldn't be honest and say what they're thinking; they should just follow the rules of institutional law and do their job. The idea of doing otherwise would be *naive* and *foolhardy*.

As expected, in the second paragraph, the author counters this view and claims there are two possible reasons why judges should, in fact, be honest and sincere. The first defense involves prudence. In short, be sincere if it will produce the best outcomes. Proponents argue this will help set an example for lower courts and give the court system legitimacy.

However, in the third paragraph, the author presents a problem with this particular argument. Morality does not justify telling the truth just because the outcome is better. The outcome is irrelevant. That leads to the other way to defend sincerity: moral principles. Judges should tell the truth because it's the right thing to do.

So, the first paragraph indeed sets the framework for the whole passage. The **Topic** is judicial opinions. The **Scope** is the question of whether judges should believe the opinions they render. The **Purpose** is to argue against the theorists. And the **Main Idea** is that judges should express what they believe—not because it's prudent, but because it's morally correct.

The author of passage B also raises the question about whether judges should believe the opinions they present. So, both passages share the same **Topic** and **Scope**, and the author of passage B quickly claims there are, indeed, reasons why judges should believe their stated opinions. Thus, the **Purpose** of passage B is to argue in favor of judicial honesty.

The second paragraph details the author's reasoning. Without such openness and honesty, judges can distort or misstate their opinions to avoid criticism, which could lead to abuse of power. Rules and laws don't matter if judges can just say anything. *Moreover*, the public can sense a lack of sincerity and lose faith in the judicial system.

In the third paragraph, the author makes some concessions: Such candor is probably not an unshakable obligation, and deception may be okay in some cases. *But*, the author stands firm and argues that a lack of honesty can be disastrous for

the legal institution. And that alone confirms the author's **Main Idea**: There is support for the use of judicial candor.

14. (B) Global

Step 2: Identify the Question Type
The question asks for something both authors seek to answer, which means the answer will address the scope of both passages. As this encompasses the entirety of each passage, this is a Global question.

Step 3: Research the Relevant Text
Don't go back into the passage. Instead, consider the Topic and Scope of both passages as determined while reading.

Step 4: Make a Prediction
Both passages had the same Topic and Scope: They talk about judicial opinions and focus on whether judges need to believe what they say when presenting those opinions.

Step 5: Evaluate the Answer Choices
(B) is correct.

(A) is a Distortion. Both authors do bring up constraints (lines 28 and 39), but they're only brought up in relation to judicial sincerity. The general idea of strengthening constraints is not a primary focus of either author.

(C) is a Distortion. While both arguments address the effect on legal institutions, the authors are not directly seeking to address that issue.

(D) is Extreme for passage A and Out of Scope for passage B. The author of passage A says transparency can help litigants (lines 17–19), but never argues that it's necessary. And the benefit to litigants is not addressed in passage B.

(E) is Out of Scope for passage A and a Distortion for passage B. Only passage B brings up costs and benefits. And that's just one point at the end. The overall focus of both passages is on judging the appropriateness of judicial candor, not weighing the costs versus the benefits.

15. (B) Inference

Step 2: Identify the Question Type
The question asks for something both authors "allude to," making this an Inference question.

Step 3: Research the Relevant Text
The question specifically asks about what the lack of candor "might affect." Passage A is mostly general ideas, but the proponents in lines 16–20 provide some effects of judicial candor. And the second and third paragraph of passage B are filled with details on the effects of a lack of candor.

Step 4: Make a Prediction
Because passage A discusses fewer specific effects, start there. According to that author, judicial candor can "provide better guidance to lower courts" and "strengthen the

institutional legitimacy of the courts" (lines 17–20). That implies that a lack of candor can affect guidance to lower courts and can hurt institutional legitimacy. The author of passage B does not mention guidance to lower courts, but does claim that lack of candor could result in "large institutional losses that would result from a lack of trust" (lines 56–57). So, the correct answer will address the effect on the legal institution as a whole.

Step 5: Evaluate the Answer Choices

(B) is a match.

(A) is Out of Scope. Neither author addresses public compliance with any judgments.

(C) is only brought up in passage B (lines 58–59), not in passage A.

(D) is only brought up in passage A (lines 17–19), not in passage B.

(E) is only brought up in passage B (lines 45–48), not in passage A.

16. (C) Logic Reasoning (Point at Issue)

Step 2: Identify the Question Type

The question asks for something about which both authors are "most likely to disagree." This will work exactly like a Point at Issue question like those found in Logical Reasoning.

Step 3: Research the Relevant Text

There are no Content Clues or line references, so the entire text is relevant.

Step 4: Make a Prediction

In general, the authors agree: Judicial candor is a good thing. Any disagreement will come down to minor discrepancies. In the third paragraph of passage A, the author argues that judges have a duty to be honest for moral reasons, not because they're trying to achieve the best outcome. In the third paragraph of passage B, the author says candor is "[p]robably not" an obligation, but should be considered when benefits outweigh the costs. In short, the author of passage A is more steadfast in pushing the moral duty of being candid, while the author of passage B allows for exceptions.

Step 5: Evaluate the Answer Choices

(C) is correct. The author of passage A agrees with this in saying that the duty to be candid is independent of producing good outcomes (lines 24–28). Passage B disagrees, saying candor does not reject the notion that lying is okay in order to yield a benefit (lines 51–55). In other words, producing a good outcome may, in fact, affect whether candor is justified.

(A) is Out of Scope. Neither author addresses partial belief.

(B) is Out of Scope. Neither author addresses the need for public debate.

(D) is Out of Scope for passage B. The author of passage A implies that telling the truth is a moral obligation, in or out of the legal system. However, passage B makes no mention of any moral obligation and never addresses truth-telling outside of the court system.

(E) is Out of Scope for passage A and a Distortion for passage B. Passage A does not address cost-benefit analysis, and passage B suggests it's important but never suggests it's *easy*.

17. (B) Logic Reasoning (Principle)

Step 2: Identify the Question Type

The question asks for a principle, making this a Principle question like those found in Logical Reasoning.

Step 3: Research the Relevant Text

The principle will support the entire argument of passage A, so use the Main Idea you summarized after reading through the passage. And make sure to also consider the Main Idea of passage B as the correct answer here should be distinct from that.

Step 4: Make a Prediction

The Main Idea of passage A is that judges should be candid because it's the moral course of action. A broader principle will apply the same logic to other behaviors: When deciding what to do, consider what's morally right. And because appealing to morality is not part of passage B, that makes it a good prediction for this question.

Step 5: Evaluate the Answer Choices

(B) matches the principle of being guided by moral considerations.

(A) is Out of Scope for passage A. Only passage B addresses debate and criticism.

(C) is Out of Scope and potentially a 180. The author doesn't discuss what's realistic or not. And as for impractical, the author suggests that the moral obligation for candor should be adhered to, regardless of the prudence or practicality of the doing so.

(D) is Out of Scope for passage A. Only passage B addresses cost-benefit analysis.

(E) is a Distortion. The author doesn't compare prudential reasons in favor of candor to prudential reasons against candor. The comparison drawn is between prudential reasons and moral reasons.

18. (D) Inference

Step 2: Identify the Question Type

The question asks for something each author *implies*, making this an Inference question.

Step 3: Research the Relevant Text

The question asks about judicial candor in general, which is addressed throughout both passages. The entire text is relevant.

Step 4: Make a Prediction

It may be tempting to look for the phrase "lack of judicial candor." However, an author could just as well talk about what having candor can do, which would imply that a lack of candor would do the opposite. A reliable prediction will be difficult here, so test the answers and make sure that the correct answer is addressed by both authors.

Step 5: Evaluate the Answer Choices

(D) is correct. The author of passage A claims that judicial candor could be justified "[i]f it can be shown that [it] produces the more prudential outcomes" (lines 12–15). However, by the third paragraph, the author claims it's not about producing good outcomes, suggesting that better outcomes may, in fact, arise without candor. And the author of passage B implies the same, by suggesting that the lack of candor may be warranted and yield a net benefit in some cases (lines 52–55).

(A) is a 180. The author of passage B implies otherwise, suggesting that judicial candor is probably not, in fact, an unshakable rule (lines 51–55).

(B) is a Distortion for passage A and Out of Scope for passage B. The author of passage A says that candor would provide "better guidance to . . . litigants" (lines 18–19), but that doesn't mean a lack of candor would be insufficient. It just wouldn't be as good. Besides, passage B never addresses the effect on litigants.

(C) is Extreme. Both authors advocate for candor, but neither says a lack of candor is *unavoidable*.

(E) is only suggested in passage B (lines 48–50), not in passage A.

19. (E) Detail

Step 2: Identify the Question Type

The question asks for something "mentioned in" the passage, making this a Detail question.

Step 3: Research the Relevant Text

There are no research clues, so the correct answer could use any random detail from throughout passage B.

Step 4: Make a Prediction

There are lots of details in passage B that are not in passage A, e.g., diluting constraints on judges' power (lines 38–40), criticism and condemnation (line 42), abuse of power (line 45), public detection of lack of candor (lines 48–50), and cost-benefit analysis (lines 55–59). Rather than combing through and predicting every example possible, it might be better to test the answer choices individually.

Step 5: Evaluate the Answer Choices

(E) is correct. Such restraints are mentioned in lines 44–45, but never in passage A.

(A) is a 180. This is mentioned in lines 5–6 of passage A, not in passage B.

(B) is Out of Scope. Neither author addresses the possibility of unintentional deception.

(C) is a 180. The question of transparency is the main focus of both passages.

(D) is a 180. Only passage A addresses guidance to litigants (lines 17–19).

20. (E) Logic Reasoning (Point at Issue)

Step 2: Identify the Question Type

The question asks for something about which both authors are "most likely to disagree," making this a Point at Issue question like those found in Logical Reasoning.

Step 3: Research the Relevant Text

Because there are no Content Clues or line references, the entire text is relevant.

Step 4: Make a Prediction

In general, the authors agree that judicial candor can be good. Any disagreement will come down to minor discrepancies. In the third paragraph of passage A, the author argues that judges have a duty to be honest for moral reasons, not because they're trying to achieve the best outcome. In the third paragraph of passage B, the author suggests deception may be warranted in some cases, but candor should be considered when benefits outweigh the cost. In short, the author of passage A is more steadfast in pushing the moral duty of being candid, while the author of passage B allows for exceptions.

Step 5: Evaluate the Answer Choices

(E) is correct. The author of passage B would agree with this, suggesting it's okay to overrule candor when it can yield a net benefit. The author of passage A would disagree, suggesting the moral duty to tell the truth cannot be overruled.

(A) is a 180. Directly, only passage B raises the importance of people trusting the honesty of judges (lines 55–59). However, the author of passage A does present evidence that honesty can strengthen the legitimacy of the courts (lines 19–20), which suggests potential agreement, not disagreement.

(B) is only discussed in passage B. Passage A offers no opinion about debate's effect on judicial power.

(C) is a potential 180. The argument in lines 3–7 suggests that judges have to balance a number of considerations. While the author of passage A rebuts the overall idea of withholding honesty, there's no dispute that there are many considerations at hand. And the discussion of cost-benefit assessment in passage B suggests equal agreement about the many considerations at hand.

(D) is Out of Scope. Neither author addresses prudential considerations for "nonlegal situations."

21. (C) Logic Reasoning (Parallel Reasoning)

Step 2: Identify the Question Type
The question asks for a claim "most analogous to" one made in the passage. That makes this a Parallel Reasoning question like those found in Logical Reasoning.

Step 3: Research the Relevant Text
The question directly refers to a specific claim in the second sentence of the second paragraph of passage B (lines 43–48).

Step 4: Make a Prediction
The claim in the passage is that candor is a requirement of all other constraints on abuse of power, because those constraints mean nothing if judges don't have to be candid. In short, there are factors that may be important (e.g., constitutional limitations and precedents), but there's one factor (candor) that is necessary for all of them. The correct answer will take that same logic of having one essential factor and apply it to another topic.

Step 5: Evaluate the Answer Choices
(C) is a match. There are important factors in science, such as relevance and sufficiency. However, accuracy is the essential prerequisite for all such factors, just as candor was said to be essential for all constraints in judicial situations.

(A) does not match. There's nothing in the initial claim about sample groups and having proper representation to avoid bias.

(B) does not match. There is no one factor that is a prerequisite for all of the constraints mentioned. Instead, it only talks about success despite those constraints.

(D) does not match. This raises the ethical nature of an action, not how such an action is required for all other actions.

(E) does not match. It pushes the importance of honesty, but does not match the idea that honesty is required for all other factors involved in the situation at hand.

Passage 4: The Fall of Grand Theories

Step 1: Read the Passage Strategically
Sample Roadmap

Line #	Keyword/phrase	¶ Margin notes
3	marked by	Grand theories defined
8	for example	Freudianism
11	Similarly	Marxism
16	so influential	
17	challenging	
18	tantamount to denying	
19	however	
20	tarnished	
22	discredited	Grand theories worked for their time, but they're limited, not universal
24	It is not	
26	implausible	
27	but that	
28	revealed	
29	inherent; limitations	
30	rather than	
31	Despite the decline	
35	discarding	
36	seem to have lost faith	
37	But while we no longer believe	People still desire satisfaction of inevitability
39	we still long for	
41	discomfort	
42	But; no bad thing	Auth: hopes lack of universal laws leads to consideration of historical contingency
44	hence	
47	Perhaps what is needed	
50	Rather than	
52	might instead explain	Constraints not limitations
56	In short	

Discussion

The passage begins by describing "grand theories" (Topic). These are 19th- and early 20th-century ideas that provide a "single, ambitious explanation" for a range of historical events. Examples are provided, and the author claims these theories suggest history is subject to "universal and necessary laws."

According to the second paragraph, some intellectuals vehemently defended these theories at the time; *however*, they have since fallen out of favor. The author lists reasons why: Some events didn't fit the theories; the theories were occasionally tied to political systems that failed; and the theories merely reflected the thinking of a particular era rather than universal truths.

In the third paragraph, the author notes how some people miss those theories. Getting rid of them means accepting that history is not predetermined and is not a logical product of universal laws, and that can make people uncomfortable. *But*, the author finally voices an opinion and argues that it's okay to be a little uncomfortable. That will allow people to stop vainly looking for one inevitable theory and instead consider the prospect of historical contingency. Instead of forcing a single explanation for every event, people can study random, particular events and develop new perspectives that provide a clearer vision of how history has progressed.

So, the last paragraph clears up the broader theme of the passage. The Scope is the decline of grand theories and the effect that has on current historical views. The Purpose is to explain the decline and the after effects. The Main Idea is that grand theories have fallen out of favor, supporting the idea that history is not determined by universal laws and allowing for a new perspective that accounts for historical contingency.

22. (D) Global

Step 2: Identify the Question Type
The question asks for the "main point" of the entire passage, making this a Global question.

Step 3: Research the Relevant Text
There's no need to go back into the passage. Just consult the Main Idea as determined while reading the passage.

Step 4: Make a Prediction
The Main Idea is that grand theories are no longer as popular as they once were, and that allows people to focus on a new perspective that relies on historical contingency rather than historical determinism.

Step 5: Evaluate the Answer Choices
(D) is an accurate summary of the main point.

(A) is a Distortion. The historians never discuss the complexity of 20th-century events, and this ignores the

potential move toward viewing history as historically contingent.

(B) is a Distortion and likely a 180. The theories were deterministic, but they were "products of their era" (lines 28–29) and were thus probably adequate for explaining that time period. Besides, this ignores other problems and fails to address the move toward a more historical contingent perspective.

(C) is too narrow. This concentrates too much on the problems of some grand theories and completely leaves out the end of the passage, which describes how the decline of such theories allows for a new historical contingent perspective.

(E) is far too narrow. The fact that grand theories provided some satisfaction is noted, but this ignores the broader theme of discussing the decline of grand theories and the introduction of new perspectives.

23. (C) Inference (Author's Attitude)

Step 2: Identify the Question Type
The question asks for the "author's attitude," which makes this an Inference question.

Step 3: Research the Relevant Text
While the "nostalgia for determinism" is mentioned in line 32, the author's opinion doesn't begin until line 37.

Step 4: Make a Prediction
In lines 37–41, the author concedes that losing determinism can lead to discomfort. However, in lines 42–47, the author expresses relief and that the discomfort from losing determination can *finally* help people give up the "vain hope for inevitability." So, the author understands why people are nostalgic, but realizes that it's futile to hold on to that nostalgia.

Step 5: Evaluate the Answer Choices
(C) matches the author's attitude.

(A) is a Faulty Use of Detail. Some of the original theories may have had ties to repressive political systems (lines 22–24), but the author does not apply that concern to modern people who are nostalgic for those theories.

(B) is Extreme and Out of Scope. The author does not show disdain. And while nostalgia and sentimentality are often linked, the author makes no such suggestion here and never mentions any "lack of originality."

(D) is a 180. The author seems more optimistic, suggesting that the discomfort from that nostalgia may finally result in a new perspective. There's no indication the author is fearful.

(E) is a 180. The author is excited about the prospect of contemplating contingency. The author would certainly not want to limit such contemplation.

24. (C) Global

Step 2: Identify the Question Type
The question asks for the "organization of the passage" as a whole, making this a Global question.

Step 3: Research the Relevant Text
To determine the organization, consult the margin notes rather than rereading the content of the passage.

Step 4: Make a Prediction
The first paragraph describes "grand theories." The second paragraph describes the problem with those theories. The third paragraph describes how their decline helps encourage new perspective. The correct answer will adhere to this surface-level progression.

Step 5: Evaluate the Answer Choices
(C) is a match, describing the protracted discussion of the mistake behind grand theories (their insistence on being deterministic) and the ensuing discussion of a new perspective (historical contingency).

(A) is a 180. The passage does start off describing the theories, but the second paragraph is all about the flaws, including how there are events that do *not* accurately match the theories.

(B) is a 180. The author does explain the decline of such theories, but hardly defends them. Instead, the author supports their decline and encourages replacing them with theories that rely on historical contingency.

(D) is a Distortion. The opening paragraphs describe grand theories and their shortcoming, but don't really provide a summary of their history. And the last paragraph doesn't speculate on their future. Instead, the author speculates on new theories.

(E) is only a distorted view of the first paragraph. It completely leaves out the decline of such theories and the author's discussion of new perspectives in the final paragraph.

25. (B) Logic Function

Step 2: Identify the Question Type
The phrase "in order to" helps identify this as a Logic Function question.

Step 3: Research the Relevant Text
While the question refers to a concept in line 39, it's more important to consider the context of the surrounding text.

Step 4: Make a Prediction
The concept of "cognitive satisfaction" is part of the first half of the third paragraph, before the author shifts the focus to new perspectives. In the first half of the paragraph, the author is discussing how some people are still nostalgic for deterministic theories, and the desire for "cognitive

satisfaction" is part of the reason why some people have that nostalgia.

Step 5: Evaluate the Answer Choices
(B) matches the purpose of explaining why some people are still nostalgic for determinism.

(A) is a Faulty Use of Detail. The author discusses the vain hope for inevitability, but never says why it's vain. It just is. And people's desire for cognitive satisfaction wouldn't explain that, anyway.

(C) is a 180. The author claims we "still long for cognitive satisfaction." There's no suggestion that such longing has declined.

(D) is a Faulty Use of Detail. Unrepeatable events aren't mentioned until later in the paragraph (lines 49–50). Furthermore, the author suggests that studying such events can, indeed, allow for "narrative satisfaction" (line 54).

(E) is a Distortion. The longing for cognitive satisfaction is used to show why some people continue to be nostalgic for determinism, not why they're losing interest and moving on. That's caused by the discomfort from losing belief in inevitability.

26. (D) Detail

Step 2: Identify the Question Type
The correct answer will describe something mentioned directly in the passage, making this a Detail question.

Step 3: Research the Relevant Text
Freudianism as a grand theory is described in the first paragraph (lines 1–11).

Step 4: Make a Prediction
Freudianism is said to be an example of a grand theory, described as an "influential intellectual movement . . . that attempted to account for a broad range of historical phenomena with a single ambitious explanation."

Step 5: Evaluate the Answer Choices
(D) matches the description nearly word for word.

(A) is a Distortion. Freudianism did consider some traits to be universal, but what made it a grand theory was using those universal traits as a way to view "culture, politics, and other forms of social interaction" (lines 7–11).

(B) is a Faulty Use of Detail. In the second paragraph, it is said that grand theories were *sometimes* treated as scientific fact (lines 16–18). However, it's not stated that this definitely applied to Freudianism specifically.

(C) is a Faulty Use of Detail. Narrative satisfaction isn't mentioned until line 54, and that's not a defining attribute of grand theories.

(E) is a 180. The grand theories were all about determinism. Grand theories "did not and could not" account for particular and novel events (lines 47–50).

27. (E) Inference

Step 2: Identify the Question Type
The question asks for something that "can be inferred" and with which the author is "most likely to agree," making this an Inference question.

Step 3: Research the Relevant Text
The question is very broad with no research clues, but the author's opinion is primarily concentrated in the latter half of the third paragraph (lines 42–58).

Step 4: Make a Prediction
The best summary of the author's point is the very last line: "In short, [a perspective that includes particular, unrepeatable events] would allow for the possibility of historical explanation without viewing history as fully determined." The correct answer will be consistent with that view.

Step 5: Evaluate the Answer Choices
(E) fits the author's point of view that history need not be imposed by viewing it as fully determined (i.e., looking for universal patterns). Further, this is supported when the author claims that people can finally start developing new perspectives by abandoning the hopeless search for inevitability (lines 42–47).

(A) is a 180. The author suggests that a new perspective can, in fact, "permit us . . . narrative satisfaction" (line 54).

(B) is a 180. The author advocates for historical contingency throughout the latter half of the third paragraph.

(C) is a 180. The author suggests it's a "vain hope" to search for inevitability, i.e., universal laws of history can't be found.

(D) is a 180. Marxism and Freudianism are the kinds of grand theories that the author argues against because they possessed "inherent explanatory limitations" (line 29).

Section IV: Logical Reasoning

Q#	Question Type	Correct	Difficulty
1	Point at Issue	B	★
2	Assumption (Sufficient)	D	★
3	Role of a Statement	A	★
4	Point at Issue	C	★
5	Flaw	E	★
6	Paradox	D	★
7	Point at Issue	A	★
8	Inference	D	★
9	Flaw	B	★★★
10	Parallel Reasoning	B	★
11	Assumption (Sufficient)	C	★
12	Flaw	C	★
13	Assumption (Necessary)	A	★★★
14	Weaken	E	★★★
15	Method of Argument	B	★
16	Weaken	C	★★★
17	Principle (Identify/Strengthen)	C	★★
18	Assumption (Necessary)	C	★★
19	Flaw	A	★★
20	Strengthen (LEAST)	A	★★★★
21	Principle (Identify/Strengthen)	D	★★★★
22	Weaken	E	★★
23	Inference	C	★★★
24	Paradox	E	★
25	Parallel Flaw	E	★★★★
26	Inference	E	★★★

1. (B) Point at Issue

Step 1: Identify the Question Type
There are two speakers and the question asks for something about which both speakers *disagree*, making this a Point at Issue question.

Step 2: Untangle the Stimulus
Otto drives Rhett to work every morning and has asked Rhett to help pay for fuel. Rhett argues that he shouldn't have to pay because it doesn't cost Otto any extra money to pick him up. Barbara calls this flawed and draws an analogy. Rhett not paying for fuel would be like Rhett not paying for warm air from Barbara's house if she didn't have to pay extra for what he diverted.

Step 3: Make a Prediction
Rhett feels he doesn't have to pay Otto. The point of Barbara's absurd analogy is to say that expecting a free car ride is like expecting free warm air. Because she calls this logic *flawed*, she's implying that Rhett should not expect a free ride and should help pay Otto for the fuel costs. So, the point at issue is whether Rhett should pay Otto for fuel or not.

Step 4: Evaluate the Answer Choices
(B) is correct. The Decision Tree confirms this. Rhett would say no, he should not have to pay. Barbara would say yes, he should pay. And they do disagree on this issue.

(A) is a Distortion. The argument is about whether Rhett *should* pay Otto, not whether Otto *requires* that payment.

(C) is a 180. Rhett says no, giving Rhett a ride does not increase Otto's expenses. And Barbara doesn't dispute that. By the analogy, it would appear she agrees: It doesn't increase expenses. The real issue is whether this means Rhett should pay Otto or not.

(D) is Out of Scope for Rhett. The warm air is only part of a hypothetical analogy drawn by Barbara. Rhett never addresses the analogy.

(E) is Out of Scope. This concept is merely hypothetical and part of an analogy. Neither speaker addresses whether such a plan is possible.

2. (D) Assumption (Sufficient)

Step 1: Identify the Question Type
The correct answer will allow the classicist to reach the conclusion, *if* it is *assumed*, making this a Sufficient Assumption question.

Step 2: Untangle the Stimulus
The classicist concludes ([*t*]*hus*) that the only "true democracy" would have been in ancient Athens. The evidence is that only in ancient Athens were all political decisions made by all eligible voters, not elected representatives.

Step 3: Make a Prediction
The classicist uses the term "true democracy" in the conclusion, but never defines what that term means. The classicist assumes that "true democracy" is defined by the description of ancient Athens in the evidence: a democracy where all eligible voters make all the political decisions.

Step 4: Evaluate the Answer Choices
(D) is correct, connecting the Mismatched Concepts of "true democracy" and a system in which all political decisions are made by all voters.

(A) is Out of Scope. The number of other political systems has no bearing on whether ancient Athens constituted a "true democracy."

(B) is irrelevant. Even if public debate is necessary for democracy, it could also be necessary for other political systems. The presence of public debate in Athens would thus be no guarantee of it being a "true democracy."

(C) is a Distortion. Even if ancient Greece did have just one democratic political system, that doesn't ensure that it was a "true democracy." It could still have been a pseudo-democracy.

(E) is a Distortion. Even if most Athenians attended the debates, it's still never said what a "true democracy" is and whether debate attendance helps qualify Athens as such.

3. (A) Role of a Statement

Step 1: Identify the Question Type
The question provides a claim from the stimulus and asks for its "role in the argument," making this a Role of a Statement question.

Step 2: Untangle the Stimulus
First, mark off the claim in question: "buying home insurance makes good fiscal sense." This is found in the first half of the very last sentence. Now, break down the argument. Researchers are studying Near-Earth Objects (NEOs) to develop ways of protecting Earth from being hit by one. The author is arguing that government funding for such research is not a waste of money. As evidence, the author makes an analogy to home insurance to show how that is a similar good use of money.

Step 3: Make a Prediction
The author is using an analogy to reach the conclusion. People insure their homes for protection, and that makes sense. Similarly, research into NEOs is meant to protect Earth, so the author claims it also makes sense. The claim in question, regarding home insurance making sense, is part of the analogy that ties to the author's conclusion.

Step 4: Evaluate the Answer Choices
(A) is correct. By claiming that home insurance makes sense, that connects the analogy to NEO research so that the author

can similarly conclude that NEO research makes sense—it's not a waste of money.

(B) is incorrect. The overall conclusion is about NEO research. This claim about home insurance is merely part of an analogy to support the overall conclusion.

(C) is incorrect. The claim that home insurance makes financial sense does not define any term.

(D) is a 180. Home insurance is meant to be an analogy that is *similar* to the NEO research situation, not a contrast.

(E) is inaccurate. The argument is not designed to support this claim. The argument is meant to support the conclusion about NEO research.

4. (C) Point at Issue

Step 1: Identify the Question Type
The question asks for what two speakers "disagree over," making this a Point at Issue question.

Step 2: Untangle the Stimulus
Oscar argues that student evaluations are the best way to assess teacher performance. Bettina argues otherwise, saying students don't actually recognize a teacher's impact until years later. Instead, Bettina recommends peer evaluations as a supplement or even as a better alternative.

Step 3: Make a Prediction
Oscar and Bettina disagree about the best way to evaluate teachers. Oscar says student evaluations, while Bettina says peer evaluations. The correct answer will address this point of contention.

Step 4: Evaluate the Answer Choices
(C) is correct. The Decision Tree confirms this. Oscar says yes, student evaluations are optimal. Bettina says no, suggesting a potentially *better* alternative: peer evaluations. So, they both have an opinion about this, and they disagree.

(A) is a 180. Bettina agrees with Oscar that students can adequately judge a teacher. It just might take a few years to do so properly.

(B) is Out of Scope. Bettina perhaps agrees with this, as students might be better able to appreciate the teacher after a few years. However, Oscar has no opinion about what happens in the future. It's all about evaluating the teachers now.

(D) is a 180. Both speakers would say no, agreeing that it's not necessary to get rid of student evaluations. Oscar is definitely against that, and Bettina is open to keeping student evaluations but supplementing them with peer evaluations.

(E) is Out of Scope for Oscar. Bettina directly makes this claim, but Oscar makes no mention of or suggestion about when evaluations are or should be conducted.

5. (E) Flaw

Step 1: Identify the Question Type
The correct answer will describe why the argument is "vulnerable to criticism," common language that indicates a Flaw question.

Step 2: Untangle the Stimulus
The author concludes ([s]o) that the ability to distinguish all four tastes is completely explained by our use of taste to test for healthfulness. The evidence is that taste is the primary tool we use for testing foods.

Step 3: Make a Prediction
All of the examples provided show how people have used taste to determine whether or not a food is healthy for us. However, the author goes a little too far by claiming that this *completely* explains why we recognize the four tastes. Such extreme language indicates Overlooked Possibilities. Couldn't there be more to our tasting ability than testing for health? The correct answer will point out the author's overly ambitious claim.

Step 4: Evaluate the Answer Choices
(E) is correct. Our use of taste to test the healthfulness of foods could definitely provide *some* explanation for why we distinguish tastes, but that doesn't mean it's a *complete* explanation.

(A) is a Out of Scope. This tries to suggest a necessity versus sufficiency flaw, but nothing in the evidence is said to be necessary for anything.

(B) is an Irrelevant Comparison. The argument is not about the sense with which people more often associate foods, but how we use the sense of taste and how it can help us detect which foods are healthy.

(C) is a Distortion. This might suggest that early humans weren't 100% accurate in assessing healthfulness, but that doesn't affect the argument that our taste buds developed exclusively for testing healthfulness.

(D) is a Distortion. Even if modern humans eat a lot of new foods, the four tastes still developed in early humans and could still have been developed exclusively to test food healthfulness.

6. (D) Paradox

Step 1: Identify the Question Type
The correct answer will be something that "contributes to an explanation" of the situation described, making this a Paradox question.

Step 2: Untangle the Stimulus
A city raised the price of on-street parking in a downtown area and, surprisingly, restaurants in that area experienced an increase in sales.

Step 3: Make a Prediction

The mystery here is this: If people now have to pay more to park in the area, why are the restaurants doing *better*? One of the keys might be the author's note that restaurant customers "require short-term parking." If it's now easier for people to get short-term parking, that could explain the increase in sales. The correct answer will likely show how increased parking rates could produce that result.

Step 4: Evaluate the Answer Choices

(D) is correct. If higher parking prices result in greater turnover, that means spots can open up more frequently, making it easier for people to find the short-term parking they need to have dinner.

(A) does not help. The existence of even higher priced parking (which may have always existed) does not explain why more people are going downtown for dinner.

(B) is irrelevant. It doesn't matter how the business owners felt about the price increase. Prices increased, and restaurant sales increased. Why? This still offers no explanation.

(C) is a 180 and Out of Scope. To explain a change in sales, something else must have changed. This suggests something that did *not* change. Besides, the mystery is about increased customer sales, not staff issues.

(E) is a 180. If this is true, then higher street-parking rates should have sent people flocking to the mall where parking is free. Yet the opposite is happening. The situation is now even more mysterious.

7. (A) Point at Issue

Step 1: Identify the Question Type

The correct answer will be a claim that two speakers "disagree over," making this a Point at Issue question.

Step 2: Untangle the Stimulus

Mark argues that newspaper sales are declining because of technology. The Internet can provide instant news reports while newspapers cannot. Fatuma argues that technology is not the issue. The real problem is that newspaper conventions result in long, harder to understand articles while Internet articles are short and to the point.

Step 3: Make a Prediction

Both people agree that the Internet is a problem for newspapers. The disagreement is about *why*. Mark feels it's about speed, while Fatuma believes it's about article length. The correct answer will address this question of why the Internet is hurting newspapers.

Step 4: Evaluate the Answer Choices

(A) is correct. The Decision Tree confirms this. Mark says yes, speed is the reason. Fatuma say no, it's not speed—it's article length. And they do disagree over this claim.

(B) is Out of Scope for Mark. Only Fatuma addresses article length. Mark has no stated or implied opinion on the subject.

(C) is Out of Scope for Mark. Again, only Fatuma addresses article length. Mark has no opinion on it, stated or otherwise.

(D) is Out of Scope for Mark. Once again, this is only a concern for Fatuma. Mark neither makes nor implies any claim about conventions.

(E) is Out of Scope for Fatuma. This is a claim made by Mark. Fatuma does not dispute this claim. She only argues that it's not the reason for declining newspaper sales.

8. (D) Inference

Step 1: Identify the Question Type

The correct answer here will fill in the blank at the end of the stimulus. That claim will be supported by all of the preceding information, making this an Inference question.

Step 2: Untangle the Stimulus

The author raises a debate about what statistics teachers should teach: the theory behind statistics or how to use statistics in real life. The author compares these options to learning how to build a car versus learning how to drive a car. The final claim begins by noting that drivers don't have to learn how to build a car.

Step 3: Make a Prediction

The important step here is to understand how the car analogy relates to teaching statistics and how the final claim relates back to statistics. The car analogy makes a distinction between *building* and *driving*. Building would involve knowing what parts make up a car, and driving would involve using the car. So, "building a car" is logically similar to learning "theories underlying statistics," while "driving a car" is similar to "using statistics." In the final claim, the phrase "just as" suggests that what applies to cars should equally apply to statistics. So, swapping out equal parts, if you don't have to know how to "build a car" to "drive a car," that implies you don't have to learn "theories underlying statistics" to "use statistics."

Step 4: Evaluate the Answer Choices

(D) is correct, logically completing the analogy.

(A) is a Distortion. The analogy is about the distinction between two paths of learning, not recognizing the goals of those being taught.

(B) is also a Distortion. The distinction being compared is between theory and application, not between statistics and mathematics.

(C) is a Distortion. This makes a recommendation, which is not consistent with the first half of the last sentence. Further, this fails to relate the analogy of "building vs. driving" back to the specific ideas of "theory vs. application."

(E) is another Distortion. The analogy is meant to discuss what should be taught to students, not what's needed to be a good teacher.

9. (B) Flaw

Step 1: Identify the Question Type
The question asks why the given reasoning is *flawed*, making this a Flaw question.

Step 2: Untangle the Stimulus
The evidence involves some Formal Logic. Anywhere you find lots of gnats, you'll find geckos. And for gnats to survive in an area, the climate must be wet. It's then claimed that geckos are not where the author is, so there must not be a lot of gnats (the contrapositive of the first statement).

If	abundant gnats	→	geckos

If	abundant gnats	→	wet climate

If	~ geckos	→	~ abundant gnats

The author then concludes ([*c*]*onsequently*) that wherever the author is, the climate is not wet.

If	~ abundant gnats	→	~ wet climate

Step 3: Make a Prediction
The final piece of evidence is valid, using the contrapositive of the first claim. If geckos live in *any* environment with lots of gnats, then no geckos means no gnats. That part is fine. However, the author then uses the lack of gnats to conclude a lack of wetness, an improper negating without reversing of the second Formal Logic piece of evidence. That's the problem. The evidence dictates that gnats survive *only* in a wet climate:

If	abundant gnats	→	wet climate

However, that's not the same as saying gnats live *everywhere* there's a wet climate. A wet climate is necessary, but not sufficient. So, it's possible for an area to be wet even if there are no gnats. The author overlooks this possibility and

assumes that all wet climates will have lots of gnats. The correct answer will describe this commonly tested flaw.

Step 4: Evaluate the Answer Choices
(B) is correct, presenting the Formal Logic assumption that all wet environments have a lot of gnats. The contrapositive of this claim fits the structure of the argument: If there are not a lot of gnats, the area is wet.

(A) is a Distortion. The author never states or implies that geckos *need* a large gnat population. The logic given is this: If there *are* gnats, there are geckos. However, it's okay for there to be geckos in areas without gnats. The author makes no assumption otherwise.

(C) is Out of Scope. The argument depends on the appearance of an abundant population of gnats. Where small populations can or cannot live is irrelevant.

(D) is irrelevant. There are no geckos in the author's area, so what they eat has no bearing on the claim of wet versus dry.

(E) is irrelevant. There are no geckos in the author's area, so where geckos *can* survive has no bearing on the argument.

10. (B) Parallel Reasoning

Step 1: Identify the Question Type
The correct answer will be an argument with reasoning "most similar" to that in the stimulus. That makes this a Parallel Reasoning question.

Step 2: Untangle the Stimulus
The conclusion is that Thompson is bound to lose the election. The evidence is in two parts: 1) If Thompson appeals to moderates, he won't get enough votes, and 2) if Thompson does not appeal to moderates, he won't get enough votes.

Step 3: Make a Prediction
The structure here is pretty straightforward. The same result will occur whether a certain action is performed or not. Thus, the result is guaranteed. The correct answer will use the exact same logic.

Step 4: Evaluate the Answer Choices
(B) is correct. The same result is said to occur if an action is performed or not. (If the company moves, it will lose employees; if it doesn't move, it will lose employees.) And the conclusion is that the result is guaranteed. (The company will lose employees.)

(A) does not match. There are two different results depending on whether Chen supports or opposes the new art center. The original argument had the same result no matter what.

(C) does not match. This only describes a chain of events based on an action not being performed. There's no comparing that to what happens if the action *is* performed. If anything, the author is implying that performing the action would produce a different result, contrasting the original argument.

(D) does not match. Here, the two conditions are approving a small tax increase and approving a large tax increase. That's not the same as comparing "if X happens" and "if X doesn't happen." Further, the results are not exactly the same. A small tax increase would lead to a restored pool. A large tax increase would lead to a restored pool *and* a new rec center.

(E) does not match. The conclusion type is different (X is not needed vs. X will happen). There are two different results depending on whether Madsen supports or opposes the mall project: Either she's the spokesperson or somebody else is. And the conclusion here brings up a value judgment (success) not addressed by the evidence—something the original argument never did.

11. (C) Assumption (Sufficient)

Step 1: Identify the Question Type
The conclusion of the argument will be valid *if* the correct answer is *assumed*, making this a Sufficient Assumption question.

Step 2: Untangle the Stimulus
The author concludes (*therefore*) that Downing does not deserve praise for ratting out his business partner. The evidence is that Downing was being honest, but he was merely trying to protect himself.

If	acting out of self-interest	→	~ morally praiseworthy

And according to the initial Formal Logic rule, honesty deserves praise only if one is acting out of respect for morality.

If	morally praiseworthy	→	honest out of respect for morality

Step 3: Make a Prediction
By the Formal Logic, one deserves praise *only* when acting out of respect for morality. To conclude that Downing does *not* deserve praise, the author is implying that Downing was *not* acting out of respect for morality. However, the evidence is just that Downing was acting out of self-interest. The author is thus assuming that one who acts out of self-interest is not acting out of respect for morality.

If	acting out of self-interest	→	~ honest out of respect for morality

The correct answer may also show up as the contrapositive:

If	honest out of respect for morality	→	~ acting out of self-interest

Step 4: Evaluate the Answer Choices
(C) is correct, connecting the Mismatched Concepts of "acting out of self-interest" and "acting out of respect for morality."

(A) is Out of Scope. The argument is about what qualifies one for praise, not for condemnation.

(B) is not sufficient. Even if *some* honest actions are not praiseworthy, that doesn't necessarily mean that Downing's action is among that group. Thus, **(B)** does not guarantee the conclusion.

(D) is Out of Scope. There's no discussion of the standards referring to Downing's circumstances, so this offers no support for the conclusion.

(E) is a 180 and Out of Scope. If morality demands honesty, then it makes no sense to necessarily deny Downing praise for his honesty. Further, this specifies actions that are detrimental to one's well-being. Downing was doing the opposite: acting to preserve his own well-being.

12. (C) Flaw

Step 1: Identify the Question Type
The correct answer will be the one that "describes the flaw" in the argument, making this a Flaw question.

Step 2: Untangle the Stimulus
The professor is addressing criticism from Costa, who criticizes the professor for theories that sort artworks into period styles. Costa claims that there's no shared feature of every artwork in a given period, so it's "intellectually bankrupt" to try categorizing in that way. The professor, *however*, rejects Costa's claim by pointing out how Costa's theories assign operas to particular period styles in much the same way.

Step 3: Make a Prediction
The professor adequately exposes Costa for being hypocritical. However, Costa could just be expressing his view in a "Do as I say, not as I do" manner. In other words, Costa may be well aware he's equally guilty, but that doesn't mean he's wrong. The categorizing could still be an intellectual bankrupt venture. The professor doesn't see that and is committing an *ad hominem* flaw. The professor is rejecting Costa's claim based solely on Costa's actions, not on the merit of what Costa actually says.

Step 4: Evaluate the Answer Choices
(C) is correct. The art history professor rejects Costa's criticism merely based on Costa's actions, which can be

similarly criticized. However, being a hypocrite doesn't make Costa wrong.

(A) is Out of Scope. There is no Formal Logic and no necessary condition, so there is no committing the classic flaw of necessity versus sufficiency.

(B) is Out of Scope. Costa's criticism is of the professor's current theories and it equally applies to his own current theories. Whether those theories have always been the same or have radically changed over time is irrelevant.

(D) is Extreme. The professor argues that Costa's criticism applies to Costa's opera theories as much as it does to the professor's painting theories. However, that doesn't mean it applies to *every* type of art. Besides, the professor rejects the criticism; there's no suggestion the criticism is true.

(E) is a 180. The professor's argument is based *entirely* on how Costa's theories of opera are comparable to the professor's painting theories. So, the professor assumes theories about different types of art *can* be compared, at least in this instance.

13. (A) Assumption (Necessary)

Step 1: Identify the Question Type
The question asks for an "assumption required" by the argument, making this a Necessary Assumption question.

Step 2: Untangle the Stimulus
The columnist argues that voice-recognition programs won't accurately translate spoken words to text until they can better recognize and utilize grammar and semantics. The evidence is that such programs currently can't distinguish between homophones (e.g., their and there . . . and they're, presumably).

Step 3: Make a Prediction
The current problem involves homophones, but the columnist claims the necessary solution involves better use of grammar and semantics. The assumption will connect those Mismatched Concepts: that solving the homophone problem must involve improving recognition and utilization of grammar and semantics.

Step 4: Evaluate the Answer Choices
(A) is correct. By the Denial Test, if voice-recognition technology did *not* have to be able to recognize grammar and semantics, then there would be no need to wait for that feature. That would contradict the columnist, who must thus believe that recognizing grammar and semantics *is* necessary.

(B) is Extreme. The columnist is suggesting that the programs *need* to recognize and utilize grammar and semantics. However, that doesn't mean the columnist assumes making those improvements *will* guarantee accuracy. There could still be other issues.

(C) is not necessary. What humans can do has no bearing on what computers need to perform the same task.

(D) is a Distortion. This suggests that voice-recognition programs need to be able to distinguish between homophones to recognize grammar and semantics. That gets the logic backward. The columnist is arguing that it's recognition of grammar and semantics that's needed to distinguish between homophones.

(E) is Out of Scope. The argument is about the capabilities of voice-recognition programs, not spell check.

14. (E) Weaken

Step 1: Identify the Question Type
The question asks for something that "weakens the argument," making this a Weaken question.

Step 2: Untangle the Stimulus
The author concludes ([*s*]*o*) that music with improvisation straying far from the melody should not be called jazz. The evidence is that improvisation in early jazz never strayed far from the melody.

Step 3: Make a Prediction
The author seems to be a jazz purist, one who wants jazz to stay the way it used to be. However, times change, and a change in improvisation style does not necessarily mean the music is no longer jazz. It could just be a newer style of jazz. To weaken the argument, the correct answer should indicate that the more modern form of melody-averse improvisation can still be considered jazz.

Step 4: Evaluate the Answer Choices
(E) is correct. This suggests that, even though the newer form of improvisation is a bit different, it's still more like jazz than it is anything else. So for now, until there's a brand new category of music created, jazz is the best category available—despite the author's objection.

(A) is a Distortion. This suggests improvisation is necessary for jazz. However, that doesn't mean it's sufficient. It's possible that improvisation is necessary for other styles of music, too, and the author could argue modern songs better fit one of those styles.

(B) is irrelevant. One style of music can be influenced by another style without having to be categorized by that style. So, it's possible for these modern songs to be influenced by jazz without actually being categorized as jazz.

(C) is irrelevant. Different musicians can play different styles. So, even if these musicians played early jazz, their new music could still be categorized as a different style.

(D) is a 180. It strengthens the argument because if other styles use improvisation, that can validate the author's desire to categorize this music as something else, too.

15. (B) Method of Argument

Step 1: Identify the Question Type
This question stem is not readily identifiable. However, the correct answer will be a description of a study, and a quick scan of the choices indicates the answer will describe what the study *does*, making this a Method of Argument question. It's also possible to see this as a twist on Role of a Statement, in which the question asks for the role played in the stimulus by Heinrich's study. Whatever the label, the focus should be on *how* and *why* the study is used as opposed to what the study *says*.

Step 2: Untangle the Stimulus
The stimulus begins with an observation about ravens: They could feed off a carcass alone and have food for weeks. However, they often share carcasses with other ravens, which could be seen as altruistic. And that's where Heinrich's study comes in. In the study, a mated pair of ravens claimed a carcass for their own. A group of juvenile ravens were going to starve, so they had to band together to drive away the original pair.

Step 3: Make a Prediction
What the study shows is that, contrary to initial belief, carcass sharing is not necessarily altruistic. In this case, the juveniles shared the carcass out of necessity. They had to band together to drive off the original pair. If they didn't share, the original pair would have the carcass to themselves, and the juveniles could have starved. So, the study does confirm that ravens share, but it completely contradicts the original altruistic explanation.

Step 4: Evaluate the Answer Choices
(B) is correct. In the study, there were ravens that shared a carcass, confirming the initial observations. However, the sharing ravens banded together for self-preservation, not for altruistic reasons, which suggests a reinterpretation of previously stated opinions.

(A) is a Distortion. Heinrich did not propose the self-preservation hypothesis. Only the altruistic hypothesis was proposed at first. It was the study that revealed the potential of self-preservation.

(C) is a 180. The original theory was that ravens shared for altruistic reasons. The study contradicted that rather than confirmed it.

(D) is Out of Scope and a 180. No mention is made of the methods used for the first observations. Besides, Heinrich's studies resulted in a different conclusion.

(E) is Out of Scope. There's no indication how the original studies were performed or how much data they produced.

16. (C) Weaken

Step 1: Identify the Question Type
The correct answer will "weaken the argument," making this a Weaken question.

Step 2: Untangle the Stimulus
Historians claim that medieval European peasants were deeply religious. The author concludes ([*t*]*hus*) this is debatable, suggesting they may *not* have been religious. The evidence is that medieval European record keepers were clergy members, who are likely to be biased toward religion and could exaggerate claims of devotion.

Step 3: Make a Prediction
The author is making an *ad hominem* attack against medieval clergy members. The suggestion is that these clergy members overstated the religious devotion of peasants because the clergy members were perhaps preoccupied with religion. The author is assuming a religious bias. To weaken this argument, the correct answer should diminish the likelihood of bias.

Step 4: Evaluate the Answer Choices
(C) is correct. If the merchants and nobles were not portrayed as religious, the accounts were probably not as colored by religious bias as the author implies. If the clergy members didn't feel the need to exaggerate the piety of nobles, it seems less likely they applied such bias to peasants.

(A) is irrelevant. The author isn't claiming that clergy members wrote exclusively about religious activities. Even if they reported on some non religious activities, they still could have exaggerated the religious ones.

(B) is an Irrelevant Comparison. The argument is not about comparing peasants to other people. It's about whether or not the peasants were as religious as portrayed.

(D) is Out of Scope. The argument is not about accounts being completely reliable. It's about whether the current view regarding religious attitudes is accurate or not. Besides, there's no evidence that historians *don't* have all the relevant surviving records.

(E) is irrelevant. The amount of detail does nothing to indicate whether such details were an accurate portrayal of religious attitudes among peasants or not.

17. (C) Principle (Identify/Strengthen)

Step 1: Identify the Question Type
The correct answer will be a principle, making this an Identify the Principle question. In addition, the correct answer will help "justify the argument," making this work like a Strengthen question.

Step 2: Untangle the Stimulus
The author concludes ([*t*]*hus*) that their initial use for decoration made beads a natural choice for currency. The evidence is that many other objects (e.g., gold, silver, and

feathers) were initially used for decoration before being used as currency.

Step 3: Make a Prediction
The argument is essentially that beads make sense as currency because they have the same original use as other objects of currency, assuming that original use is a valid indicator of later use. The correct answer will express this logic in broader terms, i.e., without necessarily mentioning beads, gold, currency, decoration, and so on. In general, it makes sense for an object to serve a certain purpose if it was originally used in the same manner as other objects that serve the same purpose.

Step 4: Evaluate the Answer Choices
(C) is correct, mimicking the logic of the author's argument. Beads, originally used as decoration, are likely to have the same derivative use (currency) as gold, silver, feathers, etc., which had the same original use.

(A) is Out of Scope. The argument is based on how earlier usage (as decoration) led to later usage (as currency). There is no distinguishing which usage is ultimately *primary* and which is *secondary*.

(B) is Out of Scope. Again, the argument is about earlier versus later usage, not primary versus secondary usage. It's never mentioned which use is primary and which is secondary.

(D) is a Distortion. It's never said that beads (or any object) ceased being used for decoration when they became used as currency.

(E) is a Distortion. This suggests that the more beads were used as currency (representing value), the more they'd be used for other uses. Not only does that reverse the logic of the argument, but the author is not trying to establish such a proportional relationship.

18. (C) Assumption (Necessary)

Step 1: Identify the Question Type
The question directly asks for an assumption, and one on which the argument *depends*, making this a Necessary Assumption question.

Step 2: Untangle the Stimulus
The author argues that speaking to babies in simplified language (e.g., "See the kitty?") doesn't help children learn language. The evidence is that children whose families *don't* use that kind of language are just as good at mastering the grammar of their language.

Step 3: Make a Prediction
The children were equally good at mastering the grammar, but does that mean they were just at good at learning the language? The author must assume a connection between those Mismatched Concepts. In short, the author assumes

that mastering grammar indicates that one has learned the language.

Step 4: Evaluate the Answer Choices
(C) is correct. By the Denial Test, if there are kids who have mastered grammar but haven't really learned the language, then the author's argument is not logical. It must be true that mastering grammar is a sure sign of learning the language.

(A) is Out of Scope. Paying extra attention does not necessarily indicate whether a child is more likely to learn the language or not.

(B) is Extreme. The author is arguing that simplified speech doesn't help, but that doesn't mean it has to *impair* language learning.

(D) is a 180, suggesting that linguists believe the complete opposite of the author's argument.

(E) is Out of Scope and a 180 at worst. Vocabulary is not part of the argument here. At worst, this suggests that the children who master grammar may not be as awesome as the author suggests. If learning vocabulary is equally important, it may be easier for children to get that from hearing sentences in simplified language.

19. (A) Flaw

Step 1: Identify the Question Type
The correct answer will describe how the argument is "vulnerable to criticism," making this a Flaw question.

Step 2: Untangle the Stimulus
The medical researcher is arguing that back belts don't help prevent injuries. The evidence is that employees at Flegco who use back belts are more likely to be injured than those who don't.

Step 3: Make a Prediction
Whenever two groups of people are compared, an author typically assumes they are equal in all relevant respects except for the one being compared. In this case, the researcher is comparing the employees who wear back belts to the ones who don't, assuming that all other factors are equivalent. However, it's said that all the people "lifting heavy objects" at work wear back belts. If the people who don't wear back belts spend all day sitting in padded chairs handling paperwork, then they would certainly have fewer back injuries. The people lifting heavy objects are at a much greater risk and could have had more injuries without the belt. The comparison is unfair, and the correct answer will expose that flaw.

Step 4: Evaluate the Answer Choices
(A) is correct.

(B) is an Irrelevant Comparison. It doesn't matter how Flegco employees compare to other companies' employees. The comparison is between using the back belt and not using it.

(C) is a Distortion. While the back belts are associated with more back injuries, the researcher is not assuming the back belts are *causing* the injuries. The researcher merely argues they aren't helping.

(D) is a Distortion. The claim is that back belts are correlated with more back injuries. There is no claim that back belts do *not* contribute to any effect. And there is no conclusion or suggestion that anything causally prevents something else. On the contrary, the conclusion is that back belts do *not* prevent injuries.

(E) tries to apply the flaw of necessity versus sufficiency. However, back belts are never described as sufficient. Instead, they are suggested to be *insufficient*. And nothing is said about whether back belts or any other factors are necessary or not.

20. (A) Strengthen (LEAST)

Step 1: Identify the Question Type
For this question, four choices will "strengthen the argument," making this a Strengthen question. However, the correct answer will be the one that LEAST strengthens. Don't think this means the correct answer will strengthen the argument but only to a minor degree. It will not strengthen the argument—period. It will either weaken the argument or just be irrelevant.

Step 2: Untangle the Stimulus
The author concludes ([*t*]*hus*) that Shakespeare probably learned about Euripides's *Alcestis* from a Latin translation. The evidence is that Shakespeare didn't really know Greek and thus probably didn't read the original play.

Step 3: Make a Prediction
That Greek was not a strong language for Shakespeare is decent evidence that he didn't read the original *Alcestis*. However, there's no evidence that he would have read a *Latin* translation. The author makes two assumptions: 1) Shakespeare knew Latin, and 2) Shakespeare did not use another translation, e.g., English. Four choices will validate these assumptions. The correct answer will contradict them or do nothing to support them.

Step 4: Evaluate the Answer Choices
(A) is correct. For one thing, this only says that Latin phrases appear in "a number of his plays," but does not confirm they appear in *The Winter's Tale*. Further, the Latin phrases he did use are said here to have been "widely used in England," suggesting he may not have really known Latin; he just recognized common phrases. (Just as people who use the phrase *c'est la vie* don't necessarily speak French.)

(B) does strengthen the argument. This suggests there was an English translation, but that Shakespeare probably didn't use it because it was too different from Shakespeare's play. That

makes it more likely Shakespeare based his play on a different translation, e.g., a Latin one.

(C) does strengthen the argument. This indicates that there was a Latin translation available to Shakespeare at the time he wrote his play.

(D) does strengthen the argument. This indicates that Shakespeare likely studied Latin, making it reasonable that he would have sought out a Latin translation.

(E) does strengthen the argument. This indicates that Shakespeare had used Latin translations before, so using a Latin translation of *Alcestis* would not be unusual.

21. (D) Principle (Identify/Strengthen)

Step 1: Identify the Question Type
The correct answer will be a *principle*, making this an Identify the Principle question. Further, the correct answer will help *justify* the argument given, which makes this similar to a Strengthen question.

Step 2: Untangle the Stimulus
The critic argues that it's unsurprising how the food at Traintrack Inn is lower in quality than that at Marva's Diner. The reasoning is that Traintrack is in a better location that practically guarantees customers.

Step 3: Make a Prediction
The critic is suggesting that, by having a more convenient location, Traintrack Inn doesn't have to worry as much about the food. That assumes Traintrack Inn isn't really trying because it already knows it's going to get customers. The correct answer will be a general rule that validates this assumption.

Step 4: Evaluate the Answer Choices
(D) is correct. This suggests that, if businesses don't need to attract more people, they don't have to provide better products. And that supports the critic's implication about Traintrack Inn: It's in a great location that guarantees customers, so it has no need to provide food that's better than "fairly ordinary."

(A) is a 180. Traintrack Inn gets a steady supply of customers even without improving its food. All it needs is a great location.

(B) is Out of Scope. The critic's argument is about food quality, not how to get more customers.

(C) is a 180. Traintrack Inn is more popular despite having lower quality food. The critic is suggesting a convenient location is more important than quality of food.

(E) is Extreme. The critic suggests there may be things that supersede food quality when determining popularity—i.e., location. However, that doesn't mean there is *no* relationship between food quality and popularity. Perhaps a restaurant in as good of a location as Traintrack, and with better food, is even *more* popular. So, **(E)** may explain why Marva's Diner is not necessarily popular, but it doesn't explain why Traintrack is more popular.

22. (E) Weaken

Step 1: Identify the Question Type
The question asks for something that "most seriously weakens" the argument, making this a Weaken question.

Step 2: Untangle the Stimulus
The conclusion is that higher produce prices have led to people planting personal gardens. The evidence is that two seed companies sold more seeds last year as produce prices spiked.

Step 3: Make a Prediction
There are a couple of problems with this argument. First, it commits the classic flaw of causation versus correlation. The increased produce prices and the increased sale in seeds happened at the same time (a correlation), but that's not evidence that the produce prices were the *cause* of increased seed sales. Further, the conclusion suggests that more people are planting personal gardens. However, there's actually no evidence that people are planting more personal gardens. There's only increased seed sales, and only at two companies. Maybe the seeds aren't being used for personal gardens. Or maybe those two companies are selling more seeds while other companies are selling far fewer seeds. The newspaper is overlooking a lot of possibilities, and the correct answer will suggest that produce prices are *not* leading to a boom in personal gardens.

Step 4: Evaluate the Answer Choices
(E) is correct. If a large retail seed company went out of business, then the two companies mentioned may have increased sales merely by selling to customers who used to buy from the now-defunct company. There are no new customers planting gardens. It's just the same people buying from a new supplier.

(A) is irrelevant. The reason for high produce prices has no impact on determining whether people are planting more personal gardens.

(B) is an Irrelevant Comparison. The argument is about the increase in personal gardening, not the size of the gardens. If anything, if gardens are now smaller, then increased seed sales would suggest more gardens, which would actually *strengthen* the newspaper's argument.

(C) is a 180, at worst. This suggests an increased interest in personal gardening. And while some people may have to wait to do so as part of a community garden, there could be plenty of people who can plant personal gardens at home, and those numbers may have increased.

(D) is Out of Scope. There's no indication of whether the economy is in a downturn or not. And even if it's not, that doesn't mean personal gardening can't be popular at other times, too.

23. (C) Inference

Step 1: Identify the Question Type
The correct answer is one that "must . . . be true" based on the given statements, making this an Inference question.

Step 2: Untangle the Stimulus
The first statement is pure Formal Logic. If someone is a highly successful entrepreneur, then that person's main desire is to leave a mark on the world. The inventor then differentiates highly successful entrepreneurs from everyone else. Highly successful entrepreneurs always implement solutions when they see them, and they are the only people to do so. Everyone else is too interested in other things (i.e., leisure time or job security) to implement every solution they see.

Step 3: Make a Prediction
There are two claims about highly successful entrepreneurs, so it helps to see how they can be combined. These people are the only ones who implement every solution they see. And their main desire is to leave a mark on the world. So, if there's someone who implements every solution they see, that person could only be a highly successful entrepreneur and thus must be focused primarily on leaving a mark on the world:

If	implement all solutions	→	highly successful entrepreneur	→	main desire to leave mark

As for everyone else, they may not implement *every* solution they see. However, that doesn't mean they do nothing. And as for their main desire, it may also be to leave a mark on the world, but it could be something else, too. Remember that the correct answer must be true and should not just be merely possible.

Step 4: Evaluate the Answer Choices
(C) is correct. Highly successful people are the only ones who implement every solution they see and, for all of them, their main desire is to leave a mark on the world.

(A) is a Distortion. First, it's never actually claimed that most people are not highly successful entrepreneurs. However, even if that reasonable assumption is made, it's not that those people don't want to leave a mark on the world at all. It just isn't necessarily their *main* desire.

(B) is not supported. People who invariably implement their solutions are highly successful entrepreneurs, and there's no indication how much, if any, interest they have in leisure time or job security.

(D) is a Distortion. Highly successful entrepreneurs do implement every solution they see, so implementation is surely not impacted by any interest in leisure time or job security. However, that doesn't mean interest in leisure time or job security doesn't impact the ability to see those solutions in the first place.

(E) is another Distortion. The main desire of highly successful entrepreneurs is to leave a mark on the world, not to implement their solutions to problems. So, anyone whose main desire is to implement solutions is not a highly successful entrepreneur. And there's no suggestion that all such people would actually leave a mark on the world.

24. (E) Paradox

Step 1: Identify the Question Type

The correct answer will "resolve the apparent discrepancy" in the stimulus, making this a Paradox question.

Step 2: Untangle the Stimulus

According to the author, the more calories people consume, the more likely they are to be overweight. *However*, even though nuts are high in calories, people who eat nuts regularly are less likely to be overweight than people who don't eat nuts.

Step 3: Make a Prediction

It nuts are so high in calories, then one would expect that eating a lot of nuts would lead to being overweight. Mysteriously, that's not happening. Why? The phrase "[a]ll else being equal" in the stimulus gives a hint. This is mysterious only if everything else is equal between people who eat nuts and those who don't. If there's another difference (e.g., people who do eat nuts just eat a lot less of everything else, or people who don't eat nuts eat a lot more of other high-calorie foods), then the discrepancy is resolved.

Step 4: Evaluate the Answer Choices

(E) is correct. This suggests that people who eat nuts don't eat foods that make them hungry. Thus, they are likely to eat less overall, which could explain their resistance to becoming overweight.

(A) is irrelevant. Even if being overweight did also depend on physical activity, there's no indication whether people who eat nuts are more or less likely than other people to burn calories through physical activity. Without that information, this offers no help in solving the mystery.

(B) is irrelevant. It doesn't matter how much it takes to make one feel full. The people who eat nuts are still taking in a high amount of calories.

(C) is irrelevant. This suggests an implication of the mystery: If people who avoid nuts are still overweight, then there's no reason to avoid nuts if you're trying to lose weight. Valid point or not, that does nothing to solve the mystery of *why* people who avoid nuts are more overweight in the first place.

(D) is a 180. If everyone is consuming the same number of calories on average, then the stimulus dictates they should be equally likely to be overweight. There's still no explanation for why nut-eaters are less overweight than other people.

25. (E) Parallel Flaw

Step 1: Identify the Question Type

The correct answer will be an argument with reasoning "most similar to that" in the stimulus. Further, that reasoning is described as *questionable*, making this a Parallel Flaw question.

Step 2: Untangle the Stimulus

The author concludes that a major earthquake is going to strike soon. The evidence is that there has recently been a series of minor tremors, and every previous major earthquake was preceded by minor tremors.

Step 3: Make a Prediction

The author commits the common flaw of necessity versus sufficiency. The evidence is that each major earthquake was preceded by minor tremors:

$$\text{If} \quad \begin{array}{c}\textbf{major}\\\textbf{earthquake}\end{array} \quad \rightarrow \quad \textbf{minor tremors}$$

However, the author improperly concludes that because there have been minor tremors, there will be a major earthquake.

$$\text{If} \quad \textbf{minor tremors} \quad \rightarrow \quad \begin{array}{c}\textbf{major}\\\textbf{earthquake}\end{array}$$

That would be treating the necessary condition of the evidence (minor tremors) as sufficient. Minor tremors could occur without setting off an earthquake. The author reversed the terms without negating. The correct answer will commit the same flaw: Claim that each occurrence of a particular event (earthquake) was preceded by a second event (tremors), then suggest that the presence of the second event will lead to the first.

Step 4: Evaluate the Answer Choices

(E) is a match. Each occurrence of one event (disease outbreaks) has been preceded by a second event (high infection rates among wildlife). The author then suggests that the presence of infection rates will lead to an outbreak. It's possible that animals can be infected without it leading to an outbreak in humans, just as tremors can occur without leading to an earthquake. So, the author flips without negating.

| If | disease outbreaks | → | high infection rates |

| If | high infection rates | → | disease outbreaks |

(A) does not match. In the original, all earthquakes were *preceded* by tremors. Here, all tropical storms become hurricanes *later*. Further, the original argument was based on the pre condition (tremors) occurring. Here, the argument is based on tropical storms *not* occurring. Whereas the stimulus was structured "If X → Y, Y → X", **(A)** is structured "If X → Y, ~X → ~Y". So, rather than flipping without negating, **(A)** negates without flipping.

(B) does not match. This is more logical. Every time there's been a lot of snow, the river has overflowed. There's a record amount of snow this year, so it makes sense to expect the river to overflow.

(C) does not match. This is also more logical. When other planets contain certain minerals, the planet was bombarded by meteors. Earth has those same minerals, so there's reason to suggest Earth was similarly bombarded. Besides being more consistent, this is unlike the original argument because it is not making a prediction based on past patterns.

(D) does not match. The logic here is also more consistent. Any time non-native species have been introduced, other species have always gone extinct. With non-native species being introduced to the Galapagos Islands, it would make sense to expect some other species to go extinct.

26. (E) Inference

Step 1: Identify the Question Type
The correct answer "must ... be true" based on the stimulus, making this an Inference question.

Step 2: Untangle the Stimulus
The stimulus consists of three Formal Logic statements, each of which uses the phrase "only if," which indicates a necessary condition. So, in order: 1) If someone is morally responsible for an action, then the action must have been performed freely.

| If | morally responsible | → | performed freely |

2) If an action is performed freely, then there must be a genuinely open alternative action.

| If | performed freely | → | open alternative |

3) If an alternative action is considered genuinely open, then that action cannot be morally wrong.

| If | open alternative | → | ~ morally wrong |

Step 3: Make a Prediction
Note how all of these statements can be combined to form one complete thought: If a person is responsible for an action, that action must have been performed freely, which means there must have been an alternative action, and that alternative must not have been morally wrong.

| If | morally resp. | → | performed freely | → | open alt. | → | ~ morally wrong |

The correct answer must be consistent with this statement, or its contrapositive, without illicitly negating or reversing any statement.

Step 4: Evaluate the Answer Choices
(E) is correct. By the logic given, for an action to be free, there must be a genuinely open alternative, which means it must not be morally wrong.

(A) reverses the logic.

| If | open alternative | → | morally responsible |

An alternative being genuinely open is necessary for a person to be responsible, not the other way around. Even if someone is *not* responsible, there could be genuinely open alternatives.

(B) is Out of Scope. The stimulus only lays out the requirements for moral responsibility. There is no indication whether moral responsibility applies most of the time or only occasionally.

(C), like **(A)** gets the logic backward. A genuinely open alternative is necessary, but the presence of such an alternative is not sufficient for (i.e., does not guarantee) moral responsibility.

(D) is a 180. According to the last claim, for an action to be genuinely open, it would have to be *not* morally wrong. So, by contrapositive, if an action *is* morally wrong, then there is *not* an alternative action that is genuinely open.

Glossary

Logical Reasoning

Logical Reasoning Question Types

Argument-Based Questions

Main Point Question

A question that asks for an argument's conclusion or an author's main point. Typical question stems:

> Which one of the following most accurately expresses the conclusion of the argument as a whole?

> Which one of the following sentences best expresses the main point of the scientist's argument?

Role of a Statement Question

A question that asks how a specific sentence, statement, or idea functions within an argument. Typical question stems:

> Which one of the following most accurately describes the role played in the argument by the statement that automation within the steel industry allowed steel mills to produce more steel with fewer workers?

> The claim that governmental transparency is a nation's primary defense against public-sector corruption figures in the argument in which one of the following ways?

Point at Issue Question

A question that asks you to identify the specific claim, statement, or recommendation about which two speakers/authors disagree (or, rarely, about which they agree). Typical question stems:

> A point at issue between Tom and Jerry is

> The dialogue most strongly supports the claim that Marilyn and Billy disagree with each other about which one of the following?

Method of Argument Question

A question that asks you to describe an author's argumentative strategy. In other words, the correct answer describes *how* the author argues (not necessarily what the author says). Typical question stems:

> Which one of the following most accurately describes the technique of reasoning employed by the argument?

> Julian's argument proceeds by

> In the dialogue, Alexander responds to Abigail in which one of the following ways?

Parallel Reasoning Question

A question that asks you to identify the answer choice containing an argument that has the same logical structure and reaches the same type of conclusion as the argument in the stimulus does. Typical question stems:

> The pattern of reasoning in which one of the following arguments is most parallel to that in the argument above?

> The pattern of reasoning in which one of the following arguments is most similar to the pattern of reasoning in the argument above?

Assumption-Family Questions

Assumption Question

A question that asks you to identify one of the unstated premises in an author's argument. Assumption questions come in two varieties.

Necessary Assumption questions ask you to identify an unstated premise required for an argument's conclusion to follow logically from its evidence. Typical question stems:

> Which one of the following is an assumption on which the argument depends?

> Which one of the following is an assumption that the argument requires in order for its conclusion to be properly drawn?

Sufficient Assumption questions ask you to identify an unstated premise sufficient to establish the argument's conclusion on the basis of its evidence. Typical question stems:

> The conclusion follows logically if which one of the following is assumed?

> Which one of the following, if assumed, enables the conclusion above to be properly inferred?

Strengthen/Weaken Question

A question that asks you to identify a fact that, if true, would make the argument's conclusion more likely (Strengthen) or less likely (Weaken) to follow from its evidence. Typical question stems:

Strengthen

> Which one of the following, if true, most strengthens the argument above?

> Which one the following, if true, most strongly supports the claim above?

Weaken

Which one of the following, if true, would most weaken the argument above?

Which one of the following, if true, most calls into question the claim above?

Flaw Question

A question that asks you to describe the reasoning error that the author has made in an argument. Typical question stems:

The argument's reasoning is most vulnerable to criticism on the grounds that the argument

Which of the following identifies a reasoning error in the argument?

The reasoning in the correspondent's argument is questionable because the argument

Parallel Flaw Question

A question that asks you to identify the argument that contains the same error(s) in reasoning that the argument in the stimulus contains. Typical question stems:

The pattern of flawed reasoning exhibited by the argument above is most similar to that exhibited in which one of the following?

Which one of the following most closely parallels the questionable reasoning cited above?

Evaluate the Argument Question

A question that asks you to identify an issue or consideration relevant to the validity of an argument. Think of Evaluate questions as "Strengthen or Weaken" questions. The correct answer, if true, will strengthen the argument, and if false, will weaken the argument, or vice versa. Evaluate questions are very rare. Typical question stems:

Which one of the following would be most useful to know in order to evaluate the legitimacy of the professor's argument?

It would be most important to determine which one of the following in evaluating the argument?

Non-Argument Questions

Inference Question

A question that asks you to identify a statement that follows from the statements in the stimulus. It is very important to note the characteristics of the one correct and the four incorrect answers before evaluating the choices in Inference questions. Depending on the wording of the question stem,

the correct answer to an Inference question may be the one that

- *must be true* if the statements in the stimulus are true

- is *most strongly supported* by the statements in the stimulus

- *must be false* if the statements in the stimulus are true

Typical question stems:

If all of the statements above are true, then which one of the following must also be true?

Which one of the following can be properly inferred from the information above?

If the statements above are true, then each of the following could be true EXCEPT:

Which one of the following is most strongly supported by the information above?

The statements above, if true, most support which one of the following?

The facts described above provide the strongest evidence against which one of the following?

Paradox Question

A question that asks you to identify a fact that, if true, most helps to explain, resolve, or reconcile an apparent contradiction. Typical question stems:

Which one of the following, if true, most helps to explain how both studies' findings could be accurate?

Which one the following, if true, most helps to resolve the apparent conflict in the spokesperson's statements?

Each one of the following, if true, would contribute to an explanation of the apparent discrepancy in the information above EXCEPT:

Principle Questions

Principle Question

A question that asks you to identify corresponding cases and principles. Some Principle questions provide a principle in the stimulus and call for the answer choice describing a case that corresponds to the principle. Others provide a specific case in the stimulus and call for the answer containing a principle to which that case corresponds.

On the LSAT, Principle questions almost always mirror the skills rewarded by other Logical Reasoning question types. After each of the following Principle question stems, we note the question type it resembles. Typical question stems:

Which one of the following principles, if valid, most helps to justify the reasoning above? (**Strengthen**)

Which one of the following most accurately expresses the principle underlying the reasoning above? (**Assumption**)

The situation described above most closely conforms to which of the following generalizations? (**Inference**)

Which one of the following situations conforms most closely to the principle described above? (**Inference**)

Which one of the following principles, if valid, most helps to reconcile the apparent conflict among the prosecutor's claims? (**Paradox**)

Parallel Principle Question

A question that asks you to identify a specific case that illustrates the same principle that is illustrated by the case described in the stimulus. Typical question stem:

Of the following, which one illustrates a principle that is most similar to the principle illustrated by the passage?

Untangling the Stimulus

Conclusion Types

The conclusions in arguments found in the Logical Reasoning section of the LSAT tend to fall into one of six categories:

1) Value Judgment (an evaluative statement; e.g., Action X is unethical, or Y's recital was poorly sung)

2) "If"/Then (a conditional prediction, recommendation, or assertion; e.g., If X is true, then so is Y, or If you an M, then you should do N)

3) Prediction (X *will* or *will not* happen in the future)

4) Comparison (X is taller/shorter/more common/less common, etc. than Y)

5) Assertion of Fact (X is true or X is false)

6) Recommendation (we *should* or *should not* do X)

One-Sentence Test

A tactic used to identify the author's conclusion in an argument. Consider which sentence in the argument is the one the author would keep if asked to get rid of everything except her main point.

Subsidiary Conclusion

A conclusion following from one piece of evidence and then used by the author to support his overall conclusion or main point. Consider the following argument:

The pharmaceutical company's new experimental treatment did not succeed in clinical trials. As a result, the new treatment will not reach the market this year. Thus,

the company will fall short of its revenue forecasts for the year.

Here, the sentence "As a result, the new treatment will not reach the market this year" is a subsidiary conclusion. It follows from the evidence that the new treatment failed in clinical trials, and it provides evidence for the overall conclusion that the company will not meet its revenue projections.

Keyword(s) in Logical Reasoning

A word or phrase that helps you untangle a question's stimulus by indicating the logical structure of the argument or the author's point. Here are three categories of Keywords to which LSAT experts pay special attention in Logical Reasoning:

Conclusion words; e.g., *therefore, thus, so, as a result, it follows that, consequently,* [evidence] *is evidence that* [conclusion]

Evidence word; e.g., *because, since, after all, for,* [evidence] *is evidence that* [conclusion]

Contrast words; e.g., *but, however, while, despite, in spite of, on the other hand* (These are especially useful in Paradox and Inference questions.)

Experts use Keywords even more extensively in Reading Comprehension. Learn the Keywords associated with the Reading Comprehension section, and apply them to Logical Reasoning when they are helpful.

Mismatched Concepts

One of two patterns to which authors' assumptions conform in LSAT arguments. Mismatched Concepts describes the assumption in arguments in which terms or concepts in the conclusion are different *in kind* from those in the evidence. The author assumes that there is a logical relationship between the different terms. For example:

Bobby is a **championship swimmer**. Therefore, he **trains every day**.

Here, the words "trains every day" appear only in the conclusion, and the words "championship swimmer" appear only in the evidence. For the author to reach this conclusion from this evidence, he assumes that championship swimmers train every day.

Another example:

Susan does **not eat her vegetables**. Thus, she will **not grow big and strong**.

In this argument, not growing big and strong is found only in the conclusion while not eating vegetables is found only in the evidence. For the author to reach this conclusion from this evidence, she must assume that eating one's vegetables is necessary for one to grow big and strong.

See also Overlooked Possibilities.

Overlooked Possibilities

One of two patterns to which authors' assumptions conform in LSAT arguments. Overlooked Possibilities describes the assumption in arguments in which terms or concepts in the conclusion are different *in degree, scale, or level of certainty* from those in the evidence. The author assumes that there is no factor or explanation for the conclusion other than the one(s) offered in the evidence. For example:

> Samson does not have a ticket stub for this movie showing. Thus, Samson must have sneaked into the movie without paying.

The author assumes that there is no other explanation for Samson's lack of a ticket stub. The author overlooks several possibilities: e.g., Samson had a special pass for this showing of the movie; Samson dropped his ticket stub by accident or threw it away after entering the theater; someone else in Samson's party has all of the party members' ticket stubs in her pocket or handbag.

Another example:

> Jonah's marketing plan will save the company money. Therefore, the company should adopt Jonah's plan.

Here, the author makes a recommendation based on one advantage. The author assumes that the advantage is the company's only concern or that there are no disadvantages that could outweigh it, e.g., Jonah's plan might save money on marketing but not generate any new leads or customers; Jonah's plan might damage the company's image or reputation; Jonah's plan might include illegal false advertising. Whenever the author of an LSAT argument concludes with a recommendation or a prediction based on just a single fact in the evidence, that author is always overlooking many other possibilities.

See also Mismatched Concepts.

Causal Argument

An argument in which the author concludes or assumes that one thing causes another. The most common pattern on the LSAT is for the author to conclude that A causes B from evidence that A and B are correlated. For example:

> I notice that whenever the store has a poor sales month, employee tardiness is also higher that month. Therefore, it must be that employee tardiness causes the store to lose sales.

The author assumes that the correlation in the evidence indicates a causal relationship. These arguments are vulnerable to three types of overlooked possibilities:

1) There could be **another causal factor**. In the previous example, maybe the months in question are those in which the manager takes vacation, causing the store to lose sales and permitting employees to arrive late without fear of the boss's reprimands.

2) Causation could be **reversed**. Maybe in months when sales are down, employee morale suffers and tardiness increases as a result.

3) The correlation could be **coincidental**. Maybe the correlation between tardiness and the dip in sales is pure coincidence.

See also Flaw Types: Correlation versus Causation.

Another pattern in causal arguments (less frequent on the LSAT) involves the assumption that a particular causal mechanism is or is not involved in a causal relationship. For example:

> The airport has rerouted takeoffs and landings so that they will not create noise over the Sunnyside neighborhood. Thus, the recent drop in Sunnyside's property values cannot be explained by the neighborhood's proximity to the airport.

Here, the author assumes that the only way that the airport could be the cause of dropping property values is through noise pollution. The author overlooks any other possible mechanism (e.g., frequent traffic jams and congestion) through which proximity to the airport could be cause of Sunnyside's woes.

Principle

A broad, law-like rule, definition, or generalization that covers a variety of specific cases with defined attributes. To see how principles are treated on the LSAT, consider the following principle:

> It is immoral for a person for his own gain to mislead another person.

That principle would cover a specific case, such as a seller who lies about the quality of construction to get a higher price for his house. It would also correspond to the case of a teenager who, wishing to spend a night out on the town, tells his mom "I'm going over to Randy's house." He knows that his mom believes that he will be staying at Randy's house, when in fact, he and Randy will go out together.

That principle does not, however, cover cases in which someone lies solely for the purpose of making the other person feel better or in which one person inadvertently misleads the other through a mistake of fact.

Be careful not to apply your personal ethics or morals when analyzing the principles articulated on the test.

Flaw Types

Necessary versus Sufficient

This flaw occurs when a speaker or author concludes that one event is necessary for a second event from evidence that the first event is sufficient to bring about the second event, or vice versa. Example:

> If more than 25,000 users attempt to access the new app at the same time, the server will crash. Last night, at 11:15 PM, the server crashed, so it must be the case that more than 25,000 users were attempting to use the new app at that time.

In making this argument, the author assumes that the only thing that will cause the server to crash is the usage level (i.e., high usage is *necessary* for the server to crash). The evidence, however, says that high usage is one thing that will cause the server to crash (i.e., that high usage is *sufficient* to crash the server).

Correlation versus Causation

This flaw occurs when a speaker or author draws a conclusion that one thing causes another from evidence that the two things are correlated. Example:

> Over the past half century, global sugar consumption has tripled. That same time period has seen a surge in the rate of technological advancement worldwide. It follows that the increase in sugar consumption has caused the acceleration in technological advancement.

In any argument with this structure, the author is making three unwarranted assumptions. First, he assumes that there is no alternate cause, i.e., there is nothing else that has contributed to rapid technological advancement. Second, he assumes that the causation is not reversed, i.e., technological advancement has not contributed to the increase in sugar consumption, perhaps by making it easier to grow, refine, or transport sugar. And, third, he assumes that the two phenomena are not merely coincidental, i.e., that it is not just happenstance that global sugar consumption is up at the same time that the pace of technological advancement has accelerated.

Unrepresentative Sample

This flaw occurs when a speaker or author draws a conclusion about a group from evidence in which the sample cannot represent that group because the sample is too small or too selective, or is biased in some way. Example:

> Moviegoers in our town prefer action films and romantic comedies over other film genres. Last Friday, we sent reporters to survey moviegoers at several theaters in town, and nearly 90 percent of those surveyed were going to watch either an action film or a romantic comedy.

The author assumes that the survey was representative of the town's moviegoers, but there are several reasons to question that assumption. First, we don't know how many people were actually surveyed. Even if the number of people surveyed was adequate, we don't know how many other types of movies were playing. Finally, the author doesn't limit her conclusion to moviegoers on Friday nights. If the survey had been conducted at Sunday matinees, maybe most moviegoers would have been heading out to see an animated family film or a historical drama. Who knows?

Scope Shift/Unwarranted Assumption

This flaw occurs when a speaker's or author's evidence has a scope or has terms different enough from the scope or terms in his conclusion that it is doubtful that the evidence can support the conclusion. Example:

> A very small percentage of working adults in this country can correctly define collateralized debt obligation securities. Thus, sad to say, the majority of the nation's working adults cannot make prudent choices about how to invest their savings.

This speaker assumes that prudent investing requires the ability to accurately define a somewhat obscure financial term. But prudence is not the same thing as expertise, and the speaker does not offer any evidence that this knowledge of this particular term is related to wise investing.

Percent versus Number/Rate versus Number

This flaw occurs when a speaker or author draws a conclusion about real quantities from evidence about rates or percentages, or vice versa. Example:

> At the end of last season, Camp SunnyDay laid off half of their senior counselors and a quarter of their junior counselors. Thus, Camp SunnyDay must have more senior counselors than junior counselors.

The problem, of course, is that we don't know how many senior and junior counselors were on staff before the layoffs. If there were a total of 4 senior counselors and 20 junior counselors, then the camp would have laid off only 2 senior counselors while dismissing 5 junior counselors.

Equivocation

This flaw occurs when a speaker or author uses the same word in two different and incompatible ways. Example:

> Our opponent in the race has accused our candidate's staff members of behaving unprofessionally. But that's not

fair. Our staff is made up entirely of volunteers, not paid campaign workers.

The speaker interprets the opponent's use of the word *professional* to mean "paid," but the opponent likely meant something more along the lines of "mature, competent, and businesslike."

Ad Hominem

This flaw occurs when a speaker or author concludes that another person's claim or argument is invalid because that other person has a personal flaw or shortcoming. One common pattern is for the speaker or author to claim the other person acts hypocritically or that the other person's claim is made from self-interest. Example:

> Mrs. Smithers testified before the city council, stating that the speed limits on the residential streets near her home are dangerously high. But why should we give her claim any credence? The way she eats and exercises, she's not even looking out for her own health.

The author attempts to undermine Mrs. Smithers's testimony by attacking her character and habits. He doesn't offer any evidence that is relevant to her claim about speed limits.

Part versus Whole

This flaw occurs when a speaker or author concludes that a part or individual has a certain characteristic because the whole or the larger group has that characteristic, or vice versa. Example:

> Patient: I should have no problems taking the three drugs prescribed to me by my doctors. I looked them up, and none of the three is listed as having any major side effects.

Here, the patient is assuming that what is true of each of the drugs individually will be true of them when taken together. The patient's flaw is overlooking possible interactions that could cause problems not present when the drugs are taken separately.

Circular Reasoning

This flaw occurs when a speaker or author tries to prove a conclusion with evidence that is logically equivalent to the conclusion. Example:

> All those who run for office are prevaricators. To see this, just consider politicians: they all prevaricate.

Perhaps the author has tried to disguise the circular reasoning in this argument by exchanging the words "those who run for office" in the conclusion for "politicians" in the evidence, but all this argument amounts to is "Politicians prevaricate; therefore, politicians prevaricate." On the LSAT, circular

reasoning is very rarely the correct answer to a Flaw question, although it is regularly described in one of the wrong answers.

Question Strategies

Denial Test

A tactic for identifying the assumption *necessary* to an argument. When you negate an assumption necessary to an argument, the argument will fall apart. Negating an assumption that is not necessary to the argument will not invalidate the argument. Consider the following argument:

> Only high schools that produced a state champion athlete during the school year will be represented at the Governor's awards banquet. Therefore, McMurtry High School will be represented at the Governor's awards banquet.

Which one of the following is an assumption necessary to that argument?

> (1) McMurtry High School produced more state champion athletes than any other high school during the school year.
>
> (2) McMurtry High School produced at least one state champion athlete during the school year.

If you are at all confused about which of those two statements reflects the *necessary* assumption, negate them both.

> (1) McMurtry High School **did not produce more** state champion athletes than any other high school during the school year.

That does not invalidate the argument. McMurtry could still be represented at the Governor's banquet.

> (2) McMurtry High School **did not produce any** state champion athletes during the school year.

Here, negating the statement causes the argument to fall apart. Statement (2) is an assumption *necessary* to the argument.

Point at Issue "Decision Tree"

A tactic for evaluating the answer choices in Point at Issue questions. The correct answer is the only answer choice to which you can answer "Yes" to all three questions in the following diagram.

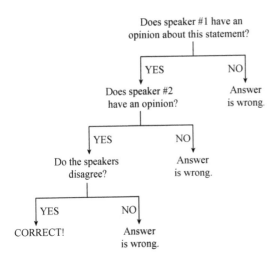

Common Methods of Argument

These methods of argument or argumentative strategies are common on the LSAT:

- Analogy, in which an author draws parallels between two unrelated (but purportedly similar) situations
- Example, in which an author cites a specific case or cases to justify a generalization
- Counterexample, in which an author seeks to discredit an opponent's argument by citing a specific case or cases that appear to invalidate the opponent's generalization
- Appeal to authority, in which an author cites an expert's claim or opinion as support for her conclusion
- Ad hominem attack, in which an author attacks her opponent's personal credibility rather than attacking the substance of her opponent's argument
- Elimination of alternatives, in which an author lists possibilities and discredits or rules out all but one
- Means/requirements, in which the author argues that something is needed to achieve a desired result

Wrong Answer Types in LR

Outside the Scope (Out of Scope; Beyond the Scope)

An answer choice containing a statement that is too broad, too narrow, or beyond the purview of the stimulus, making the statement in the choice irrelevant

180

An answer choice that directly contradicts what the correct answer must say (e.g., a choice that strengthens the argument in a Weaken question)

Extreme

An answer choice containing language too emphatic to be supported by the stimulus; often (although not always) characterized by words such as *all, never, every, only,* or *most*

Distortion

An answer choice that mentions details from the stimulus but mangles or misstates what the author said about those details

Irrelevant Comparison

An answer choice that compares two items or attributes in a way not germane to the author's argument or statements

Half-Right/Half-Wrong

An answer choice that begins correctly, but then contradicts or distorts the passage in its second part; this wrong answer type is more common in Reading Comprehension than it is in Logical Reasoning

Faulty Use of Detail

An answer choice that accurately states something from the stimulus, but does so in a manner that answers the question incorrectly; this wrong answer type is more common in Reading Comprehension than it is in Logical Reasoning

Logic Games

Game Types

Strict Sequencing Game

A game that asks you to arrange entities into numbered positions or into a set schedule (usually hours or days). Strict Sequencing is, by far, the most common game type on the LSAT. In the typical Strict Sequencing game, there is a one-to-one matchup of entities and positions, e.g., seven entities to be placed in seven positions, one per position, or six entities to be placed over six consecutive days, one entity per day.

From time to time, the LSAT will offer Strict Sequencing with more entities than positions (e.g., seven entities to be arranged over five days, with some days to receive more than one entity) or more positions than entities (e.g., six entities to be scheduled over seven days, with at least one day to receive no entities).

Other, less common variations on Strict Sequencing include:

Double Sequencing, in which each entity is placed or scheduled two times (there have been rare occurrences of Triple or Quadruple Sequencing). Alternatively, a Double Sequencing game may involve two different sets of entities each sequenced once.

Circular Sequencing, in which entities are arranged around a table or in a circular arrangement (NOTE: When the positions in a Circular Sequencing game are numbered, the first and last positions are adjacent.)

Vertical Sequencing, in which the positions are numbered from top to bottom or from bottom to top (as in the floors of a building)

Loose Sequencing Game

A game that asks you to arrange or schedule entities in order but provides no numbering or naming of the positions. The rules in Loose Sequencing give only the relative positions (earlier or later, higher or lower) between two entities or among three entities. Loose Sequencing games almost always provide that there will be no ties between entities in the rank, order, or position they take.

Circular Sequencing Game

See Strict Sequencing Game.

Selection Game

A game that asks you to choose or include some entities from the initial list of entities and to reject or exclude others. Some Selection games provide overall limitations on the number of entities to be selected (e.g., "choose exactly four of seven students" or "choose at least two of six entrees") while others provide little or no restriction on the number selected ("choose at least one type of flower" or "select from among seven board members").

Distribution Game

A game that asks you to break up the initial list of entities into two, three, or (very rarely) four groups or teams. In the vast majority of Distribution games, each entity is assigned to one and only one group or team. A relatively common variation on Distribution games will provide a subdivided list of entities (e.g., eight students—four men and four women—will form three study groups) and will then require representatives from those subdivisions on each team (e.g., each study group will have at least one of the men on it).

Matching Game

A game that asks you to match one or more members of one set of entities to specific members of another set of entities, or that asks you to match attributes or objects to a set of entities. Unlike Distribution games, in which each entity is placed in exactly one group or team, Matching games usually permit you to assign the same attribute or object to more than one entity.

In some cases, there are overall limitations on the number of entities that can be matched (e.g., "In a school's wood shop, there are four workstations—numbered 1 through 4—and each workstation has at least one and at most three of the following tools—band saw, dremmel tool, electric sander, and power drill"). In almost all Matching games, further restrictions on the number of entities that can be matched to a particular person or place will be found in the rules (e.g., Workstation 4 will have more tools than Workstation 2 has).

Hybrid Game

A game that asks you to do two (or rarely, three) of the standard actions (Sequencing, Selection, Distribution, and Matching) to a set of entities.

The most common Hybrid is Sequencing-Matching. A typical Sequencing-Matching Hybrid game might ask you to schedule six speakers at a conference to six one-hour speaking slots (from 9 AM to 2 PM), and then assign each speaker one of two subjects (economic development or trade policy).

Nearly as common as Sequencing-Matching is Distribution-Sequencing. A typical game of this type might ask you to divide six people in a talent competition into either a Dance category or a Singing category, and then rank the competitors in each category.

It is most common to see one Hybrid game in each Logic Games section, although there have been tests with two Hybrid games and tests with none. To determine the type of Hybrid you are faced with, identify the game's action in Step 1 of the Logic Games Method. For example, a game asking you to choose four of six runners, and then assign the four chosen runners to lanes numbered 1 through 4 on a track, would be a Selection-Sequencing Hybrid game.

Mapping Game

A game that provides you with a description of geographical locations and, typically, of the connections among them. Mapping games often ask you to determine the shortest possible routes between two locations or to account for the number of connections required to travel from one location to another. This game type is extremely rare, and as of February 2017, a Mapping game was last seen on PrepTest 40 administered in June 2003.

Process Game

A game that opens with an initial arrangement of entities (e.g., a starting sequence or grouping) and provides rules that describe the processes through which that arrangement can be altered. The questions typically ask you for acceptable arrangements or placements of particular entities after one, two, or three stages in the process. Occasionally, a Process game question might provide information about the arrangement after one, two, or three stages in the process and ask you what must have happened in the earlier stages. This game type is extremely rare, and as of November 2016, a Process game was last seen on PrepTest 16 administered in September 1995. However, there was a Process game on PrepTest 80, administered in December 2016, thus ending a 20-year hiatus.

Game Setups and Deductions

Floater

An entity that is not restricted by any rule or limitation in the game

Blocks of Entities

Two or more entities that are required by rule to be adjacent or separated by a set number of spaces (Sequencing games), to be placed together in the same group (Distribution games), to be matched to the same entity (Matching games), or to be selected or rejected together (Selection games)

Limited Options

Rules or restrictions that force all of a game's acceptable arrangements into two (or occasionally three) patterns

Established Entities

An entity required by rule to be placed in one space or assigned to one particular group throughout the entire game

Number Restrictions

Rules or limitations affecting the number of entities that may be placed into a group or space throughout the game

Duplications

Two or more rules that restrict a common entity. Usually, these rules can be combined to reach additional deductions. For example, if you know that B is placed earlier than A in a sequence and that C is placed earlier than B in that sequence, you can deduce that C is placed earlier than A in the sequence

and that there is at least one space (the space occupied by B) between C and A.

Master Sketch

The final sketch derived from the game's setup, rules, and deductions. LSAT experts preserve the Master Sketch for reference as they work through the questions. The Master Sketch does not include any conditions from New-"If" question stems.

Logic Games Question Types

Acceptability Question

A question in which the correct answer is an acceptable arrangement of all the entities relative to the spaces, groups, or selection criteria in the game. Answer these by using the rules to eliminate answer choices that violate the rules.

Partial Acceptability Question

A question in which the correct answer is an acceptable arrangement of some of the entities relative to some of the spaces, groups, or selection criteria in the game, and in which the arrangement of entities not included in the answer choices could be acceptable to the spaces, groups, or selection criteria not explicitly shown in the answer choices. Answer these the same way you would answer Acceptability questions, by using the rules to eliminate answer choices that explicitly or implicitly violate the rules.

Must Be True/False; Could Be True/False Question

A question in which the correct answer must be true, could be true, could be false, or must be false (depending on the question stem), and in which no additional rules or conditions are provided by the question stem

New-"If" Question

A question in which the stem provides an additional rule, condition, or restriction (applicable only to that question), and then asks what must/could be true/false as a result. LSAT experts typically handle New-"If" questions by copying the Master Sketch, adding the new restriction to the copy, and working out any additional deductions available as a result of the new restriction before evaluating the answer choices.

Rule Substitution Question

A question in which the correct answer is a rule that would have an impact identical to one of the game's original rules on the entities in the game

Rule Change Question

A question in which the stem alters one of the original rules in the game, and then asks what must/could be true/false as a result. LSAT experts typically handle Rule Change questions by reconstructing the game's sketch, but now accounting for the changed rule in place of the original. These questions are rare on recent tests.

Rule Suspension Question

A question in which the stem indicates that you should ignore one of the original rules in the game, and then asks what must/could be true/false as a result. LSAT experts typically handle Rule Suspension questions by reconstructing the game's sketch, but now accounting for the absent rule. These questions are very rare.

Complete and Accurate List Question

A question in which the correct answer is a list of any and all entities that could acceptably appear in a particular space or group, or a list of any and all spaces or groups in which a particular entity could appear

Completely Determine Question

A question in which the correct answer is a condition that would result in exactly one acceptable arrangement for all of the entities in the game

Supply the "If" Question

A question in which the correct answer is a condition that would guarantee a particular result stipulated in the question stem

Minimum/Maximum Question

A question in which the correct answer is the number corresponding to the fewest or greatest number of entities that could be selected (Selection), placed into a particular group (Distribution), or matched to a particular entity (Matching). Often, Minimum/Maximum questions begin with New-"If" conditions.

Earliest/Latest Question

A question in which the correct answer is the earliest or latest position in which an entity may acceptably be placed. Often, Earliest/Latest questions begin with New-"If" conditions.

"How Many" Question

A question in which the correct answer is the exact number of entities that may acceptably be placed into a particular group

or space. Often, "How Many" questions begin with New-"If" conditions.

Reading Comprehension

Strategic Reading

Roadmap

The test taker's markup of the passage text in Step 1 (Read the Passage Strategically) of the Reading Comprehension Method. To create helpful Roadmaps, LSAT experts circle or underline Keywords in the passage text and jot down brief, helpful notes or paragraph summaries in the margin of their test booklets.

Keyword(s) in Reading Comprehension

Words in the passage text that reveal the passage structure or the author's point of view and thus help test takers anticipate and research the questions that accompany the passage. LSAT experts pay attention to six categories of Keywords in Reading Comprehension:

Emphasis/Opinion—words that signal that the author finds a detail noteworthy or that the author has positive or negative opinion about a detail; any subjective or evaluative language on the author's part (e.g., *especially, crucial, unfortunately, disappointing, I suggest, it seems likely*)

Contrast—words indicating that the author finds two details or ideas incompatible or that the two details illustrate conflicting points (e.g., *but, yet, despite, on the other hand*)

Logic—words that indicate an argument, either the author's or someone else's; these include both Evidence and Conclusion Keywords(e.g., *thus, therefore, because, it follows that*)

Illustration—words indicating an example offered to clarify or support another point (e.g., *for example, this shows, to illustrate*)

Sequence/Chronology—words showing steps in a process or developments over time (e.g., *traditionally, in the past, today, first, second, finally, earlier, subsequent*)

Continuation—words indicating that a subsequent example or detail supports the same point or illustrates the same idea as the previous example (e.g., *moreover, in addition, also, further, along the same lines*)

Margin Notes

The brief notes or paragraph summaries that the test taker jots down next to the passage in the margin of the test booklet

Big Picture Summaries: Topic/Scope/Purpose/Main Idea

A test taker's mental summary of the passage as a whole made during Step 1 (Read the Passage Strategically) of the Reading Comprehension Method. LSAT experts account for four aspects of the passage in their big picture summaries:

Topic—the overall subject of the passage

Scope—the particular aspect of the Topic that the author focuses on

Purpose—the author's reason or motive for writing the passage (express this as a verb; e.g., *to refute, to outline, to evaluate, to critique*)

Main Idea—the author's conclusion or overall takeaway; if the passage does not contain an explicit conclusion or thesis, you can combine the author's Scope and Purpose to get a good sense of the Main Idea.

Passage Types

Kaplan categorizes Reading Comprehension passages in two ways, by subject matter and by passage structure.

Subject matter categories

In the majority of LSAT Reading Comprehension sections, there is one passage from each of the following subject matter categories:

Humanities—topics from art, music, literature, philosophy, etc.

Natural Science—topics from biology, astronomy, paleontology, physics, etc.

Social Science—topics from anthropology, history, sociology, psychology, etc.

Law—topics from constitutional law, international law, legal education, jurisprudence, etc.

Passage structure categories

The majority of LSAT Reading Comprehension passages correspond to one of the following descriptions. The first categories—Theory/Perspective and Event/Phenomenon—have been the most common on recent LSATs.

Theory/Perspective—The passage focuses on a thinker's theory or perspective on some aspect of the Topic; typically (though not always), the author disagrees and critiques the thinker's perspective and/or defends his own perspective.

Event/Phenomenon—The passage focuses on an event, a breakthrough development, or a problem that has recently arisen; when a solution to the problem is proposed, the author most often agrees with the solution (and that represents the passage's Main Idea).

Biography—The passage discusses something about a notable person; the aspect of the person's life emphasized by the author reflects the Scope of the passage.

Debate—The passage outlines two opposing positions (neither of which is the author's) on some aspect of the Topic; the author may side with one of the positions, may remain neutral, or may critique both. (This structure has been relatively rare on recent LSATs.)

Comparative Reading

A pair of passages (labeled Passage A and Passage B) that stand in place of the typical single passage exactly one time in each Reading Comprehension section administered since June 2007. The paired Comparative Reading passages share the same Topic, but may have different Scopes and Purposes. On most LSAT tests, a majority of the questions accompanying Comparative Reading passages require the test taker to compare or contrast ideas or details from both passages.

Question Strategies

Research Clues

A reference in a Reading Comprehension question stem to a word, phrase, or detail in the passage text, or to a particular line number or paragraph in the passage. LSAT experts recognize five kinds of research clues:

Line Reference—An LSAT expert researches around the referenced lines, looking for Keywords that indicate why the referenced details were included or how they were used by the author.

Paragraph Reference—An LSAT expert consults her passage Roadmap to see the paragraph's Scope and Purpose.

Quoted Text (often accompanied by a line reference)—An LSAT expert checks the context of the quoted term or phrase, asking what the author meant by it in the passage.

Proper Nouns—An LSAT expert checks the context of the person, place, or thing in the passage, asking whether the author made a positive, negative, or neutral evaluation of it and why the author included it in the passage.

Content Clues—These are terms, concepts, or ideas from the passage mentioned in the question stem but not as direct quotes and not accompanied by line references. An LSAT expert knows that content clues almost always refer to something that the author emphasized or about which the author expressed an opinion.

Reading Comp Question Types

Global Question

A question that asks for the Main Idea of the passage or for the author's primary Purpose in writing the passage. Typical question stems:

Which one of the following most accurately expresses the main point of the passage?

The primary purpose of the passage is to

Detail Question

A question that asks what the passage explicitly states about a detail. Typical question stems:

According to the passage, some critics have criticized Gilliam's films on the grounds that

The passage states that one role of a municipality's comptroller in budget decisions by the city council is to

The author identifies which one of the following as a commonly held but false preconception?

The passage contains sufficient information to answer which of the following questions?

Occasionally, the test will ask for a correct answer that contains a detail *not* stated in the passage:

The author attributes each of the following positions to the Federalists EXCEPT:

Inference Question

A question that asks for a statement that follows from or is based on the passage but that is not necessarily stated explicitly in the passage. Some Inference questions contain research clues. The following are typical Inference question stems containing research clues:

Based on the passage, the author would be most likely to agree with which one of the following statements about unified field theory?

The passage suggests which one of the following about the behavior of migratory water fowl?

Given the information in the passage, to which one of the following would radiocarbon dating techniques likely be applicable?

Other Inference questions lack research clues in the question stem. They may be evaluated using the test taker's Big Picture Summaries, or the answer choices may make it clear that the test taker should research a particular part of the passage text. The following are typical Inference question stems containing research clues:

It can be inferred from the passage that the author would be most likely to agree that

Which one of the following statements is most strongly supported by the passage?

Other Reading Comprehension question types categorized as Inference questions are Author's Attitude questions and Vocabulary-in-Context questions.

Logic Function Question

A question that asks why the author included a particular detail or reference in the passage or how the author used a particular detail or reference. Typical question stems:

The author of the passage mentions declining inner-city populations in the paragraph most likely in order to

The author's discussion of Rimbaud's travels in the Mediterranean (lines 23–28) functions primarily to

Which one of the following best expresses the function of the third paragraph in the passage?

Logic Reasoning Question

A question that asks the test taker to apply Logical Reasoning skills in relation to a Reading Comprehension passage. Logic Reasoning questions often mirror Strengthen or Parallel Reasoning questions, and occasionally mirror Method of Argument or Principle questions. Typical question stems:

Which one of the following, if true, would most strengthen the claim made by the author in the last sentence of the passage (lines 51–55)?

Which one of the following pairs of proposals is most closely analogous to the pair of studies discussed in the passage?

Author's Attitude Question

A question that asks for the author's opinion or point of view on the subject discussed in the passage or on a detail mentioned in the passage. Since the correct answer may follow from the passage without being explicitly stated in it, some Author's Attitude questions are characterized as a subset of Inference questions. Typical question stems:

The author's attitude toward the use of DNA evidence in the appeals by convicted felons is most accurately described as

The author's stance regarding monetarist economic theories can most accurately be described as one of

Vocabulary-in-Context Question

A question that asks how the author uses a word or phrase within the context of the passage. The word or phrase in question is always one with multiple meanings. Since the correct answer follows from its use in the passage, Vocabulary-in-Context questions are characterized as a subset of Inference questions. Typical question stems:

Which one of the following is closest in meaning to the word "citation" as it used in the second paragraph of the passage (line 18)?

In context, the word "enlightenment" (line 24) refers to

Wrong Answer Types in RC

Outside the Scope (Out of Scope; Beyond the Scope)

An answer choice containing a statement that is too broad, too narrow, or beyond the purview of the passage

180

An answer choice that directly contradicts what the correct answer must say

Extreme

An answer choice containing language too emphatic (e.g., *all*, *never*, *every*, *none*) to be supported by the passage

Distortion

An answer choice that mentions details or ideas from the passage but mangles or misstates what the author said about those details or ideas

Faulty Use of Detail

An answer choice that accurately states something from the passage but in a manner that incorrectly answers the question

Half-Right/Half-Wrong

An answer choice in which one clause follows from the passage while another clause contradicts or deviates from the passage

Formal Logic Terms

Conditional Statement ("If"-Then Statement)

A statement containing a sufficient clause and a necessary clause. Conditional statements can be described in Formal Logic shorthand as:

If [*sufficient clause*] → [*necessary clause*]

In some explanations, the LSAT expert may refer to the sufficient clause as the statement's "trigger" and to the necessary clause as the statement's result.

For more on how to interpret, describe, and use conditional statements on the LSAT, please refer to "A Note About Formal Logic on the LSAT" in this book's introduction.

Contrapositive

The conditional statement logically equivalent to another conditional statement formed by reversing the order of and negating the terms in the original conditional statement. For example, reversing and negating the terms in this statement:

> **If   A   →   B**

results in its contrapositive:

> **If   ~B   →   ~A**

To form the contrapositive of conditional statements in which either the sufficient clause or the necessary clause has more than one term, you must also change the conjunction *and* to *or*, or vice versa. For example, reversing and negating the terms and changing *and* to *or* in this statement:

> **If   M   →   O AND P**

results in its contrapositive:

> **If   ~O OR ~P   →   ~M**